The American Empire

By

Brendan James Magee

And

A.C. Underwood II

September, 2009

"No one can be a slave of two masters;

He will hate one and love the other;

He will be loyal to one and despise the other.

You cannot serve both God and money..."

Matthew 6:24

THE AMERICAN EMPIRE

Table of Contents

OPENING STATEMENT

My partner and I have noticed with concern some serious changes, which have come over our country (USA). It is hard to depict exactly when these changes all began, but they did, and are now a part of American life, threatening the public safety and well-being. We view these changes as causing an epidemic of fear, which has gradually seeped into American society. Parents are afraid to allow their children to go to the local playground alone or go out after dark. There are sections of the city nice people don't visit, especially late at night. Driving on any roads or highways is dangerous due to a possible car collision; even occurring a short distance from one's home. Going into a convenience store can be dangerous, if there is a robbery taking place at the time, and they happen more often than they should. A pedestrian crossing the street is increasingly at risk from a speeding motorist. In certain neighborhoods older people aren't safe in their own homes from breaking and entering and robbery. The list goes on and on, and as such prompted our interest. This book is a result of that interest.

We decided to format the work with essays; each one concentrating on a particular subject, which we feel has contributed to the average American's loss of their civil liberties. Yes, that's how we view these changes, and have made it a challenge for the book to uncover.

The work depicts the American people: their personality, how they think from their entitlement principles on to their sense of morality or lack thereof. We view it all on a cause and effect basis. Next we look to history for how it all began. Our belief is, it all started in the nineteen sixties and carried on from there to the nineteen eighties, which we feel was also a key time in the development of the nation to what it is today. What we discovered from our research was quite surprising. Our nation is more than a super power; it is an empire, and secondly there is a correlation between the emergence of the Empire, and the average citizen's loss of their civil liberties.

Our overall mission in writing the book is to educate the reader on what the average American lost. If by doing so, it shows the American Empire in an unfavorable light, then so be it. We make no excuses for how revealing the work turns out to be.

- NOTE: My partner is related to me by blood, acts as my legal counsel, and has been a consultant writer on this book.

End of: OPENING STATEMENT

AMERICAN STYLE

Americans love to spend money. They are the ultimate consumers, who buy whether they have the money or not, content to be in debt the rest of their lives as long as they get what they want. For this writing we are limiting this contention to our countrymen. Since no man is an island, no nation is either, especially with global trade becoming more prevalent in the new century. If this is so, and I have no reason to doubt it, the American buying craze, most likely, is spreading overseas. What effect this will have on the broader economic situation is open for speculation. Consequently, our thinking told us to limit ourselves to a study of the USA economy, which may give us a clue about the worldwide economy of the future and what to expect.

When times are good and most people are working, Americans are a spending group of consumers, and practice this down to their last dime. This is good and bad. Good because demand pumps up the economy. Bad, because

Americans don't always purchase the right products and services, and don't always buy intelligently. They are influenced by fads and advertising, which exploits this extraordinary desire to purchase what everybody else is buying. God knows, who determines this; there is a head dog somewhere setting the course for everyone to follow. Whoever is setting the pace, however, doesn't always have concern for morality, and what is good for the environment, as is evidenced by the black market drug sales and the vast popularity of the oversized passenger SUV's and vans, which are adding more than their share of polluting gases, and endangering the safety of the roads we travel.

This isn't to say that Americans aren't interested in the environment. They are, or they think they are, but not enough to give up their fads. As a matter of fact, one of their fads has to do with the environment: the typical American will be interested in the tail end of consuming – trash collecting and recycling. It is a way for them to settle their conscience about their insatiable appetite for buying the wrong commodities, which aren't always environmental friendly. Their local community's regulations on separating the trash to assist the recycling effort is an opportunity to do this. Of course, we shouldn't forget to assist a large recycling business somewhere, which will make someone rich. This becomes the problem: the recycling effort is money driven. For example, more money can be made on the sale of an SUV than on a small compact car. The fact that the larger vehicle pollutes the air more is of little concern, because the fad makers and advertisers are only interested in profits, not humanity.

Therefore, the fads persist, the fad makers dictate, and the thought is ingrained deeply into the American's mind set: "we must separate our junk accordingly – cans in one container, plastic in another, paper in another." They do so religiously, twice a week; satisfied, they are, "greening America – saving the planet." They (generally speaking) don't realize the so called "greening" comes at a price: dumping polluting fertilizers and other chemicals on their lawns, will eventually make its' way into streams and waterways polluting them, and killing the life they support. Another misconception is: the various filters their gas guzzling oversized vehicles have on them, neutralize the poisonous, exhaust gases which run through the engines. This just isn't so.

At best, if functioning properly, these filters may take care of perhaps fifty percent of them; the larger the vehicle, the more poisons it produces. The gases are responsible for smog and global warming, which are greatly interfering with weather patterns and the delicate balance of the world's ecosystem. Average Americans don't think about this, because no one tells them about it; they only do what they are told to do. Don't get me wrong, recycling is good, but it is not enough. When are the fad makers going to get around to telling Americans that they should buy less polluting smaller cars? It sounds sensible to me: look at the money the average citizen will save, which can go into buying other commodities, or savings for their children's college education.

Note: For further information concerning the environment, we offer our book entitled: Everything You Should Know About The World's Environment But Are Indifferent To Ask!

With morality Americans are similarly misdirected into a complacent belief of no-belief. They are convinced that like the environment, they know everything there is to know about it. A shrinking percentage of them still go to Mass and Holy Communion or their synagogue or church meeting, sometimes. They really don't have to, because they know everything there is to know about being good. This being the case, leaves the Sabbath as an open day for them to sleep late, do household chores, wash their SUV's (god number 1), play with their computer (god number 2), watch the ball game on their television in the back yard and annoy the neighbors (their third and fourth gods). It's not that they don't believe in the living God; they do in a way, but they believe more in other gods, so they worship them on Sunday, and don't go to church. Besides, they don't need to go there, because they are good people, and don't need anybody preaching to them about something they already know everything about. If you don't believe me, ask them. I have.

Americans in general believe they are kind and fair to one another. This is one of their fads, strengthened by their educational training, which dictates that the living God doesn't exist. Teachers are strictly forbidden to even postulate that there may have been an ultimate cause. So, as far as morality is concerned, the book is open, and one can invent their own morality. That is exactly what Americans do. Their morality is essentially what the group accepts as right. It goes something like this: they speak regularly with their neighbors, and draw from them what is the current acceptable thinking of the neighborhood. This fills them in on the in-people, and how they think. Once they are clued in on the going trends, they can operate accordingly. For example if a neighbor has a falling out with another neighbor, he can, through the local gossip, systematically destroy that neighbor's reputation. They don't look on it this way; it is considered a warning about a bad person, who isn't bad, but since they operate outside what is considered normal and correct, they receive a reputation. The terms used against them are vague: he is aggressive and peculiar and overly protective of his property. Usually what this means is, he had at one time approached an in-person about their kids playing on his newly planted lawn or some such trivial matter. Instead of accepting the correction, and telling their brats to respect other people's property, they take the gossip route as a form of revenge. Nobody can tell them what to do. "Who do they think they are anyway?" This is an American for you: you can't tell them they are wrong, since they don't take correction well, or at all. They have their minds made up ahead of time, and will react aggressively to most situations, defending themselves and their children, even when it is clear they are wrong.

Even though Americans don't understand morality, they do know what "push and shove" is all about, and use these bullying tactics as a way of thinking to make some buying decisions. Take for example, a typical way an American solves a fear problem. He is aware of the many accidents and violence on the highways. Motivated by his fear and concern for the safety of his family, the American reacts by buying a large SUV, with a battering device mounted on the front, so he, his wife and children can be safe in the event of an accident. Confident no harm will come to them, while driving this rig, they go around aggressively tailgating and bullying other motorists with smaller cars. The American doesn't take the high road (no pun attended) in solving the problem by practicing safe driving habits, and being polite to other drivers on the highway. Instead, he buys the dangerously made, converted pickup truck, the manufacturers dub an SUV or Sports Utility Vehicle, and adds more to the dangers of highway motoring.

Economically, taking the SUV fad as an example, it has the following impact on the country. One, the vehicle uses about three times the amount of petroleum than the average compact car; two, since the vehicle is larger, it adds to the congestion on the roads and streets, which causes more accidents and traffic delays; three, by consuming more gas, the SUV makes the USA dependency on foreign sources increase significantly for oil supply, which pushes up the cost at the pump, and tips the balance of payments for the country as a whole; four, the larger SUV by burning more fuel, adds greatly to air pollution and comparable diseases attributed to this contamination (as noted before).

The rationale for the larger auto is, it protects the inhabitants more in the event of a collision, and consequently is worth all the economic pressure placed on the economy by the expense and fuel consumption. In other words, bigger is better, but is it? Statistics indicate this isn't necessarily so. SUV's have a ten percent higher accident rate than the average car. The speculation for this poor safety record is how aerodynamically the vehicle is built: its' height and narrow wheel base don't provide the proper stability built into it to maintain control under certain adverse highway conditions. From the outset of its' manufacture in the late eighties and all through the nineties into the new century, nothing was done by the government or manufacturers to protect the citizens from this design flaw. It took the six largest auto makers in the world to get together, and decide to build a safer SUV vehicle on their own. The reason they did this wasn't morality driven, but because of the number of lawsuits they received and also because these vehicles were unsafe. The jury is still out on their success, since the changes were only recently put into effect.

Although I agree with what the manufacturers did, I still hold reservations that the changes will solve the problem, since I don't believe the danger of these vehicles lies solely in their design. My gut feeling tells me differently.

The hazards with the SUV are more with the type drivers, who buy such machines. They appear to me to be people, who easily give way to fear and anger.   These drivers are lulled into a false sense of security, as mentioned before; they believe no one can hurt them in their little tank, and consequently take unnecessary chances. With an attitude like that, no design change will improve the auto's safety record. As of now there is no car or truck on the road, which provides total safety to the driver and passenger(s). The fact of the matter is a highway nightmare which has gotten worse with the advent of the SUV. Americans use this as their answer to road hazards. Ironically, they used one hazard to correct another.

To elaborate more on safety, it is going away, the most important element in the driving equation, and should be the main motivation of the manufacturer and consumer alike. The average American's belief that more weight and power, together with more speed in their vehicle, will answer the safety problem, is foolish. The old saying, "two wrongs don't make a right," answers this postulation.

It is not only wrong, but it makes matters worse.

Instead, why not build a vehicle, which is well made with steel reinforced doors and a stronger passenger compartment. Make it smaller, designed to handle adverse highway conditions, and provide its' driver with maneuverability and automatic characteristics, which react to hazardous impulses of other motorists, such as driving too close and cutting-out the other car. The American's desire to out muscle their fellow countrymen on the road is romanticizing bullying, and is getting away from the main purpose of the motor car: to provide safe, dependable transportation. Why should a passenger vehicle go one hundred twenty miles per hour; can't you get there at half that speed?   The technology is available to do all of the above. The only question is, "where are our priorities?"

Note: We will devote an entire chapter later on in the book concerning Road Safety, and go over some of the above suggestions in more detail.

Now with all volatile spending economies, the problem of inflation is always omnipresent, and should always be in the minds of all concerned in the supply/demand process. Let's examine how it can be brought to bear, limiting our example to a significant price increase change in a typical consumer's purchase of a key product, such as the family car. This important purchase is where the wisdom of the consumers becomes important. When the consumer decides, for whatever fad prompts them to do so, to pay almost double for a vehicle, and likewise the maintenance and upkeep of it, then inflation or some such economic collapse is probable. An example of this can be viewed through personal income (or P. I.), which obviously is limited. When more of it goes into one product, and its' resulting services and associated products, then it can't go into another. To clarify this, personal Income being dominated by transportation related products and services can't go into buying clothes, home repairs, entertainment, education and so forth. This is called the hierarchy of demand. Changes in consumer buying habits can affect other industries and businesses, causing plant shut downs and unemployment. This is always a threat with a free enterprise economy. We say this cautiously, because it is difficult to predict economic issues accurately. Many changes and unforeseen catastrophes affect it.

Personal Income and the Hierarchy of Demand are good tools to use, when making such an attempt, since they deal with consumer buying habits. As with all habits, they are subject to change. Look out for these changes; they will direct you to where the economy is going. Let's just conclude our theory by simply saying, "all things being equal," the above could take place.

We haven't forgotten the supply side of the economy. Before getting too involved with it, I want to digress somewhat and lead into it with a few comments about Advertising and the Marketing approach to selling. In business school, my professor, a part time teacher, was an advertising company executive in his day job. He possessed a rather cocky attitude, which was annoying, and further aggravated by the fact that he seemed to cater to a couple of students, who worked for him in his advertising firm. His attitude, as I later would find out, was stimulated by a deep belief the industry he represented could affectively influence demand. By the time his two courses were over, he proved this to me. In a nutshell this is what he taught me: if you keep telling your market how good a product or service you offer is, they will in time believe it. When the consumer is ready to make a buying decision, he will make it with your company's name in his head. I'm not going into the many media available to the advertiser. I'm sure all of these are familiar to you, since you are a consumer. My point here is, don't take advertising for granted. It is a multi-billion dollar business for a reason. It can and does every day influence your buying decisions, no matter how unbelievable the commercials appear to be.

America is a free enterprise society, which up to this point in our history, has been successful for the most part. The major flaw with such an economy is a tendency for its' major industries to drift into bigness. Although our country has anti-trust laws, they have largely been ignored by various Presidents in recent years, causing buyout frenzies in various key industries. As a result, massive companies have emerged, and with them a serious breach of the competitive drive of a free economy has followed. The consumer is left with a product, which is thrust on him by the advertising marketing machine and uncaring executives. They represent suppliers, who are giant companies, controlling whole industries with the power to fix prices, which they do, without any government interference. Take for example the oil industry, controlled by four companies. They simply, through interlocking directorates which run these corporations, fix prices. Their profits are enormous; they are the only show in town. If you want to drive your car, and you have to, since our country is a car society, you have to pay their prices. This is a great deal of power for a small group of directors, controlling this industry. Theodore Roosevelt, our 26th President, warned about bigness in business back in the early 20th century in his efforts to control the Trusts of that time. The Trusts were, what we now call Monopolies (one), or Oligopolies (few). They were a group of men, who essentially tried to corner the market of a particular commodity(s). President Roosevelt's concern was that no organization or group should be more powerful than the Presidency. One must at least entertain such a thought. Are the oil industry, the insurance industry, the automobile industry, the banking industry stronger than the Presidency? Here we are faced with greed against greed. Credit buying, uninformed consumers, and giant suppliers are acting irresponsibly for the better interest of the nation. What do we all have to show for it? We are faced with economic collapse, which has resulted in a massive loss of jobs, a record number of home foreclosures, a failure of financial institutions, etc. Just as the country was faced with the Great Depression of the nineteen thirties, it is now encountering the same economic deterioration. Both, I believe, were caused by the same greed factors between consumers and suppliers.

Note: This "bigness" problem will also be discussed later in the Reagan chapter.

Now when the economy fails, it fails suddenly and rapidly, much like a snow ball rolling down a hillside, collecting momentum, as it goes along. In time, it is affecting everything in its path, including the giant corporations, since they must operate in the very economy, their greed has aided to collapse. You know the old saying, "what goes around, comes around." None of us live in a vacuum; that's why greed doesn't work. To keep profits where the corporations want them to be, they can do nothing but raise prices, and this is where inflation comes on the scene.

Life isn't always fair; it should be, but it isn't. Greed won't allow it to be. Let's examine it with regard to inflation, which we consider the forerunner of an economic downturn. Who loses the most, when it hits? It will not be the rich for they will remain in control, since they know the system and will work it, and even continue to make money. You can bet they will go to bed at night with full stomachs. You know the old saying, "the rich get richer." What about the middle class, will they get clobbered by the inflationary spiral? After all they were the main group, who were responsible for triggering the increases in the first place. Surprisingly, no, since they are in a position to remedy their situation with salary increases or price restructuring according to the expense of the times. They appear to get by, after they adjust, and buy smaller more sensible cars, and stop acting greedy for the present. Here they are provided for in the system, because they are the people who run it. When they are out of business, the system will be too.

Then what group does inflation hurt the most? It stands to reason, the people with marginal income or fixed incomes have the most to lose under run-away inflation, since they have no way to make up for the price increases for the necessities that are needed to live on and survive. They are the sickly, the poor and the old, who make up the forgotten citizens of our affluent land. Doesn't seem right, does it? Through fear and greed, we as a nation set off a spiral of avarice which forges on down the economic order of our citizenry, until it hits bottom and can go no further. The inflation malfunction ends, where it always has in the history of mankind: with the poor.

Note: We will go over the American economy in greater detail in the Supply and Demand chapter.

If our American style is to succeed, it is imperative that consideration be added to it, for its' lower class. History has shown over and over, a society without compassion towards its' poor is destined to fail. To remedy this, greed in the market place between suppliers and consumers must come under control. Believe me there is enough supply to go around, and yes we are our brother's and sister's keeper.

There is more to the average American's morality issues, and we will be introducing them to you, as we go along in the book. For now, greed is a good beginning, since it is at the heart of America's difficulties, especially at home.

End of   AMERICAN STYLE

THE MONEY COUNTRY

There are only two capitalistic countries in the world: Switzerland and the United States of America. Many of the more economically stable countries are socialistic, where the various phases of the economy such as the natural resources, basic industries, banking and credit are nationalized by the government. Switzerland and the USA are money driven by supply and demand and a free enterprise economy. Switzerland is a nice place to visit, but not of major consequence to the world's economy. The USA on the other hand is. In fact, America probably impacts every nation's economy the world over. The US dollar has few rivals; it can buy anything in any market anywhere a plane or boat can take you. Try doing that with a Ruble or Euro.

Now if you are an American, it is easy to be proud of our accomplishments in the area of making money, and I am. However, there are some things which go on in our land, puzzling me and at times disappointing me. If our country is so economically sound, you would think everything should be good for all of us, wouldn't you? But, is it? Do all our citizens have what they need? Is poverty abolished? Is crime under control? Can anyone receive a college education? Can every one of us have a nice home, enough food to eat every day, a car to drive around in, clothes on our backs, medical care, and so forth?

Do we Americans run the money machine, or does it run us? What do we get out of this great economy, which we all helped create? I'll repeat my question in a different way: does everybody receive the same medical benefits, education, protection under the law, a steady job when we are older, and early retired? Or, is it that some Americans benefit by the money machine; the group who have money? It doesn't take much brain power to figure this out. Since our country is money driven, it is the wealthy Americans who have the nice homes, the fine cars, eat the good food, get the right education for their children, and receive justice in the courts of law. Is this equality? Of course it isn't. I would not be troubled with this fact of life, if there were a trend in the country to improve the lower middle class and poor people's situation, allowing them to advance.   This is shrinking, instead of improving. That's the rub.   Don't talk to me about Affirmative Action; it has been around for a long time in many American institutions and industries, and has failed miserably.   The policy is simply another form of discrimination.   Using discrimination to solve a discrimination problem, doesn't make sense.

For the less fortunate, and this group appears to be growing faster than the fortunate, there is less.   For example, welfare, social security and Medicare are dwindling in real value. Education costs are rising much faster than the inflationary rate.   Medical care insurance is less available for our large middle class. The HMO's, which many citizens are on today, don't provide the care that was provided by the Blue Cross/Blue Shield medical insurance furnished forty years ago, which paid all costs to the physician of your choice.   What happened?   Why is it that the stronger our nation becomes economically, the less the average person has to show for it?   Who's getting the money?   Why is it, when I was a boy the average family relied on one income; now the average family can't get by without two salaries coming into the home?

I wasn't always this cynical. There was a time, when I blamed myself for not becoming rich. Where did I go wrong? Why didn't I go out, and grab the bull by the horns, and get my share of the money which is so available in this great money country of ours? Doggedly, my blame centered on myself for my quite normal financial position, which appeared to be my path in life. Not once did my thinking ever conceive the possibility that it wasn't my fault. Not once did I even dare think, maybe the money out there is taken up by a certain number of people, who obtained it before I had a chance to get any of it. Maybe all the green backs are all tied up with them, the money people of the money country. No, no that can't be the truth. What if it is the truth? Just suppose it might be. The thought crossed my mind after losing two low paying jobs, which weren't enough to pay all my bills, as I went out on my own. I was living with my parents back then. The thought persisted: what do I do about getting some of the money from the money people; assuming it is possible to pry it from their grubby little hands? I remained confident that I could, regardless of my two prior failures.

Perhaps if I give it a little more thought, and plan out my approach to making money, my opportunities would improve. What I needed was a game plan; you know what the pro football teams had. I began to think in the terms of making a good living, not becoming rich. First off, I didn't want to operate outside the law. This eliminated numerous possibilities, such as stealing, extortion, dealing with illegal black market drugs and the like. Since I had little stomach for this sort of thing, I had to limit myself to honest employment. My reasoning was to work with one of the large corporations, since they had a great deal of money, and some of them had a good reputation for being fair to their workers. Perhaps some of it would trickle down to me, if I was conscientious enough and proved my loyalty. I believed that hard work would be appreciated by such a company, and it would be rewarded by them in the long term. This wasn't a good idea. After devoting thirty six years to one very rich firm, they decided, worker productivity wasn't a priority; they only cared about early retirement. So here I am with my social security, a modest pension and a wife, who (thank God) has earning potential.

I tried to get a job, but the best available for me was a crossing guard position, which has certain fulfilling advantages, but making money isn't one of them.

Here, I'm getting a little ahead of myself. As part of my separation package, the company provided their executives (me) with the assistance of a management placement service. The service furnished the following: counseling, a private office, a telephone, FAX machine, a typist and mailing metering to aid its' clients in their job search. In time it became apparent that my job search and their counseling wasn't bearing much fruit. Not wanting to concede that it was close to impossible for an ex-manager in his late fifties to find a job at his previous level of employment, they suggested I go into business for myself. This didn't work, because the banks wouldn't lend me the money to get started, nor would the government; the latter only took money from me; they didn't give any. The banks said I was too old, and the government gave the excuse, I wasn't a minority. So with no money, I couldn't open my own business, and without a job I couldn't save any either. Consequently, it takes money to get money; if you don't have any, you can't get any. Oh, by the way, after a few years of not being able to find work for myself, the management placement service fired me.

It took a long time, but I was starting to figure out why so many people living in the money country didn't have any money. It was out there, but it wasn't for the taking, unless you were a thief. Not working gave me time to look into and research the American system. The management placement firm had many good books and references on the subject, and they had computers, which accessed the internet. I'll list some of these books in the bibliography. I read and studied up on the subject and learned the following. To make money, you have to go through a thing called, the Machine; some people refer to it as having connections or getting your foot in the door, or getting a break. Whatever you call it, you have to work through it, if you want to make any money. Now the Machine was put into place by the money people, who invented it to keep ordinary people from getting rich people's money. The Machine dictates, who governs the country, what information reaches the public and by what media coverage, what clothes we wear and what food we eat, what entertainment we view on the silver screen and on television, where we live and just about everything we do and think. It tells us, we are a democracy, but dictates the choices we have, and they are only two for every governmental post. Third party candidates don't usually succeed. In the end, if we work hard, the Machine will provide the normal family with just enough money to live on, and by the look of things most of us will be in debt, when they put us in the ground. The Machine says it affords everybody equal opportunity, but it is more equal to the very rich, because it takes money to make money, and of course connections.

Ironically it is the Machine, which provides the very statistics, proving their existence and control over our society. They can be quite arrogant about this, because they realize the majority of Americans don't understand the system, and are content to carry on, without challenging it. This allows the rich business people (the in-crowd) to use the statistics in planning their investments and enterprises. The data lists the various socioeconomic backgrounds, and shows how well they fare under the Machine: what salaries they make, where they live, what clothes they wear, what they eat, etc. Clearly shown through these numbers is the fact that they don't add up to the famous American Dream, which we are taught or led to believe is open to all of us. Simply put, some of us get more than others, controlled by our religious beliefs, the color of our skin, and all the old bigotries, which placed us in the order of who gets what. All men aren't necessarily created the same, as far as the Machine is concerned. For example, Black Americans with all their high paid athletes, don't on the average in other walks of life earn as much as whites, and don't live in as nice neighborhoods as whitey. There is one thing they are ahead of white people on, more blacks are in jail (on a population ratio). Also more blacks die younger than whites (from high blood pressure, diabetes and lung cancer), and the lack of preventive medicine, since they can't afford health care insurance.

I won't bore you with all the books I read at the placement service; they were quite a few, since I had time on my hands. Future employers weren't exactly ringing the phone off the hook to schedule an interview with me. The two reference books most helpful in providing statistics concerning the data in the last two paragraphs were from two almanac books:

(1) The World Almanac and Book of Facts 1999, an imprint of PRIMEDIA Reference Inc., Mahwah, NJ.

(2) TIME Almanac 2003 with Information Please – Information Please, Boston, MA – part of Family Education Network, Inc. – TIME Inc. Home Entertainment – Copyright 2002 by Education Network, Inc.

Let's address why more poor people are in jails first. Obviously the majority of inmates belong there. We aren't going to go into the police/court system at this point. It appears to be more than fair to the accused than in most societies. However, the imbalance between well off versus poor people in prison should be looked into in relation to money. Now I'm not talking about guilt here, whether they belong there or not. It is sufficient enough to assume most of the inmates belong in prison, even though they are the first to admit bad luck in being incarcerated.

Of course, many crooks are walking the streets, who belong in jail, but aren't there, nor will they ever be. The money issue remains our main concern and the topic of this paper. Why are most incarcerated people from poor backgrounds? The possibilities are given by whatever biases the giver may possess: one, most crimes are committed by poor people, because they weren't brought up right; two, lower class people are stupid, and get themselves caught easily; three, poor people don't have the money to hire the right attorney to defend themselves in court, when they do get caught. If I were a gambling man, point three is where I would put my money. Here's what an attorney told me: you can spend as much as $20,000 on legal representation defending against a felony charge. If you are from poor circumstances, where do you get this kind of money?

To support our money theory I've enlisted the aid of statistics from TIME Almanac, rating state and federal prison inmates by race, which supports our money theory. They received their data from a report by the Justice Policy Institute in 2002: the number of black men in prison has grown to five times the rate it was twenty years ago. As of 2002, more black men were in jail than in college, 791,600 versus 603,032. In 1980 there were 143,000 blacks in prison compared to 463,700 enrolled in college.

In the year 2000 the following statistics concerning Americans in prison were recorded (by race): White 36%, Black 46%, Hispanic 16%, and other 2%. Source: Prisoners in 2000, U. S. Bureau of Justice Statistics.

One other disturbing statistic from TIME has to do with the rising cost of a college education. From 1986 to 2001 the average yearly cost of a public institution went from $4,138 in 1986 to $8,655 in 2001; for private institutions costs went from $10,039 to $21,907. Tuition has doubled in a short period of time, which coincides with the jail statistics. Why? What are they doing in the universities, which warrants such increases? It seems nobody is questioning these increases. I frankly don't know. I do know this, these increases are keeping lower class young people from attending. It seems many of them have given up on a college education. Some turned their attention to crime. Petty crime is most of it, committed by petty criminals, which sometimes turns into something more serious. From here the court system becomes involved.

How it works in a court of law is the judge is impartial. He will only act on what is presented by the plaintiff and the defense attorneys. If the defense doesn't enter a good argument in behalf of his client, it will not become a part of the proceedings. The old saying, "you get what you pay for," is essentially the way the system works. With a court appointed attorney, he has little time and the necessary facilities to defend his client, compared to a large legal firm. The idea here is if you decide to be a thief, then steal big, and when you do get caught, you will be able to afford a good attorney. Therefore, the poor guy gets screwed again.

The next way he gets screwed is by the health care system. The best way to deal with a serious illness, such as cancer, heart disease, and diabetes is to catch the disorder before it gets out of hand. Regular check-ups and taking the proper treatments are the ways to deal with your health issues. Without Health Care Insurance this becomes an expensive proposition. For a large percent of the less financially able people in our population, this insurance is unaffordable.

TIME, once more, is providing statistics: Americans Without Health Insurance – White 13%, Non-Hispanic 10%, Black 19%, Asian and Pacific Islander 18%, Hispanics 32%; Household Incomes Without Insurance – less than $25,000 per year 23%, $25,000 to $49,999 17%, $50,000 to $74,999 11%, $75,000 and up 7%.   Again money is calling the shots: the more you have the better your health care.

With all these numbers in mind, we can go right to the heart of the paper's thesis, and ask, "what is more important in the Money Country: money or morality?   Don't be too quick to answer this question; think about it for a while.   When you do, ask yourself a second question: do you know what morality is?   I'm not going to tell you what it is, citing the old saying, "if you don't know, I'm not going to tell you."   Let me just say, you should know what it is, since morality is, I believe, part of a human being's make-up.   It is a most important possession in dealing with everyday obstacles a person has to face.   It is logical, comforting, rewarding and practical, even though it may not appear that way at the time you use it.

America made a huge mistake, when the founding fathers put together its' constitution. Although they advocated, "all men are created equal," the practice wasn't clearly written into the law. They instead left this decision up to the different states. As a result, many states opted to permit a terrible practice called, slavery. The judgment was made, placing money ahead of morality. The decision has haunted our country ever since, and will continue to do so for God knows how long – both races alike. It is clear, none of us live in a vacuum; we must all live and survive influenced by the mistakes of the past.

Every American, black and white alike, should study black history in our country. Why? Because it is our business to know about it, and be aware of the consequences of this error. It is better to know than not to know, since knowledge brings about understanding. I studied it in one of the colleges, I attended. It horrified me that man could do this injustice legally to man. Don't tell me this is practiced in other countries. That doesn't make it right. We're not writing about

other countries; we're writing about America.
America is better than that, or should be. Briefly,
this is what I learned at the university. A business
was formed: it consisted of a fleet of ships,
manned by a group of thugs to sail to the African
continent. Their mission was to round up as many
able bodied men and women, forcing them against
their will to be transported to the United States.
The conditions aboard their vessels were sub-
standard, and their abductors were cruel and
abusive. Many died along the way, as a result of
the bad treatment. Those, who survived, were
sold at auction like animals for their future owners
to do whatever they wanted with them. The
slaves had no rights under the law. There was
evidence that many of them were raped, beaten,
starved and branded, like a horse or steer. In
addition to this, they were bred like dogs and
horses. One slave owner would have a stud, he
took around for a fee to breed with young slave
girls. A slave youth rarely knew his father, nor did
he ever have a family life. The purpose of the
breeding was to develop a slave of superior
strength and size to be able to lift more and work
longer hours. The whole practice was a business.

It was excused as such. A slave owner satisfied his conscience by telling himself this: it is only business, and I don't mistreat my slaves. But you didn't try to stop it either!

With all this indignity and hardship, the blacks greatest loss which came out of this practice, was the loss of their culture, having been ripped away from them at the initial abduction. They worked from sun up to sunset every day. They barely had time to eat their evening meal and go to bed; let alone develop a culture. Without it the individual loses generations of learning, normally passed down from his ancestors. Culture tells a human being everything he needs to know: how to act, what to do, how to live, how to tie your shoelaces, how to go to the bathroom, how to survive in a society. A person without it, has a lot of catching up to do.

Before getting off the subject, I would like to give you one more example about money versus morality. I wasn't going to, because it has to do with the church, but I just couldn't resist. It goes something like this. Friends of mine live next to a church property. Their small back yard is directly behind a driveway leading up to the rear of the church's auditorium building. The church has various fund raising events they hold at the site, which include dining and food catering for a sizable number of their congregation. The sounds from the festivities apparently are within reason, since my friends had no reason to complain on that count. However, what did prompt their complaints happened many years later and came as a complete surprise to my friends. One day without any heads up or warning, a group of workmen showed up to pave the area near the property line with a cement slab. When asked about it by the husband, the workmen informed him that a large trash dumpster was going to be placed on the site of the slab. Evidently the church's business was picking up, and they needed a better method of getting rid of the refuse, they estimated would be accumulating as a result.

My friends were devastated. Their dream house wasn't so dreamy anymore. Nothing like smelling somebody's garbage, and listening to the large metal lid of the bright orange can being opened and shut several times during the day and sometimes at night to take away from one's home sanctity. Don't forget about the flies and other vermin that are attracted to it, as well as the dumpster being an eyesore.

I'm not an attorney; my partner is. I guess this is why they came to me with the problem. Perhaps they thought my association with him, had rubbed off on me. In any event my advice to them was to hire a good lawyer, and sue the church.

"Wait a minute," they replied in shock. "We can't sue a church. What kind of people do you think we are?"

They were indignant, that I would refer to church people in such an insulting manner, treating them as if they were like anyone else.

"Well then move," I said bluntly.

"But, but we can't do that. We lived all our lives in this house; raised our children here, the memories; how could we just get up and leave?"

"Well, that's one of your options," I replied; this time lowering my tone of voice; trying to appear more sympathetic. This is all I could tell them, so I ended the conversation, feeling sad that these two good people are being taken advantage of by a Christian organization, and what is really disappointing is the church isn't even aware they are doing something immoral, or they don't give a damn one way or the other. Both are bad.

If the church doesn't know what they are doing morally, then where does that leave us? It leaves us no longer believing in organized religion. It leaves us making up our own morality, as I said before, which is a bad place to be. The church isn't doing their job of teaching all nations. This is the tragedy of the day. Christians don't know what Christianity is; they are simply business men and women. What works for money is their number one priority; not saving their immortal souls.

Okay, what should the church do about the dumpster inconvenience to the neighbor? After all, it is tied in with their fund raising function and all the money it raises, which keeps the church afloat. Some of it actually goes to charity.

(3)Christ gave us the answer, "If you want to be perfect, go and sell all you have and give the money to the poor, and you will have riches in heaven; then come follow me." Matthew 19, 20, 21

Being a Christian is difficult. One has to sacrifice money for morality. The challenge is, can you do it.   It is easy to be wrong, so most people give into it, and tell themselves they are right, if the money is right.   Money is a bad criterion to follow, because it doesn't always equal morality.

(4)The Money Country is one of the most dangerous nations on earth in which to reside. Allow me to backup that statement with statistics: murders – 15th highest; highest per capita rate of people in prison – 737 per 100,000 or 2.2 million; 4th highest number of executions; 3rd highest rape rates; 3rd highest major assaults.

Not only is the United States dangerous to live in, it also presents dangers to other nations as well: having more forces stationed abroad (460,000 fighting persons in 144 countries). U. S. weapons and equipment are the most advanced in the world; they spend almost as much on their military as all nations combined.   The country has more deliverable nuclear weapons than anyone else, and also leads in the value of the arms sold to other governments.   Per capita military expenses rank third in the world.

(4)Source: Parade Magazine 1/14/2007

My point here is not so much in how

dangerous the USA is, but why. Why is a country with such great wealth and opportunity in it, and such a strong central government have so much human slaughter going on in its' streets and highways? This is further compounded by the open policy of transporting this violence abroad by selling sophisticated weaponry to questionable leadership in buying countries, as well as backing these sales up with a large military presence worldwide. We decided in order to understand this penchant for violence, it was best to approach it from the American love of money side. We have given examples of money being more important in the U. S. than morality. If this is true on a broad basis, then it explains quite a bit about the American's violent nature, which rises from the ordinary citizen up to the country's leadership and policy making.

Let's take a closer look at this mentality and examine an ordinary issue, which most people in other nations would deal with on peaceful terms. In America such a situation may not be handled this way. As an example, a motorist on an American highway cuts out another driver. Annoyed by what happened he pulls along–side of the aggressive driver's car at the next traffic light, draws his revolver and shoots her to death (true story). This sort of senseless violence goes on in our country, and is reported almost daily, I'm sorry to say. In studying this come-back type retaliation crime, my partner and I came to the conclusion that Americans in general somewhat deify violence, as if it were the eleventh commandment. They possess a wild-west mentality of shoot first and ask questions later. Or, should I say they are on the edge, viciously attacking another human being is something they hold as a potential right, under the proper circumstances. A typical American would never consider, "turning the other cheek." This brings me back to money and how it feeds this mentality. Money is cold, non-loving. It suggests that the owners of it must defend their ownership at any cost, even to the point of killing another human being, who is trying to take their money away from them. Or, if they feel threatened that they are going to be robbed, they will take drastic measures to protect their money. Consequently, it is reasonable to conclude a mindset of this caliber dominating a nation, would not only encourage the production of hand guns, but would support it with the needed legislation to legalize it.

The fact that the USA doesn't have effective gun legislation tells me money, not morality is the dominant credo of my country. You don't need to have much of a mind to know proper gun legislation in America would greatly reduce violence and crime within our borders. Think about it! All that's required is a few sentences, put into the US Constitution, revising it: "Hand guns and related automatic weapons are not permitted in the possession of the general population. Those in violation of this act will receive a minimum prison sentence of five years." Of course the President of the USA and the Congress would have to provide leadership and face the National Rifle Association and the lobbying large gun manufacturers. I'm only dreaming that such resolve and courage could come out of our leadership. Wouldn't it be wonderful, if they did something like this for the common good of the American people? Just imagine for a few moments, putting an end to senseless violence and destruction of human lives brought about by guns. I'll give you that time to think about it..... Yes, I know it is only a dream, but worthwhile change begins with a dream.

Another benefit of gun legislation is, it gives the police something to work with in dealing with crime. If a suspect is caught carrying a gun, it is taken from him, and he goes to jail. That's the upside of the law. The downside is, many gun manufacturers would need to retool, and produce a less deadly product as a result. How about a product, which wouldn't kill or mutilate: perhaps a stun gun. But, what excitement would there be in stunning someone? I guess that would never sell. That is the rub: selling, making money. However, change is what it is. You either work with the new way or die by it. After all, large corporations use change as an excuse, when laying off thousands of their workers. Wouldn't it be interesting to see how the large gun manufacturers deal with a change, which put them in a compromising position? Yes, I agree, change is inevitable, and gun legislation will become a fact of life someday (no pun intended). I'm not a bleeding heart liberal, when I predict and support this. In fact I don't even know what a bleeding heart liberal is. I do know that it is looked down on in this country and somehow put into the American value system as a weak person, who gives way to the bad guy and the interests of the American Empire. I'm not for either. I'm on the side of common sense, which clearly is telling me that my country has a serious gun control problem within its borders. Like it or not, this is the twenty first century, not 1776. "The right to bear arms," clause in the Constitution doesn't have the same meaning, it had back when the country was founded. This stubborn adherence to an outdated law is doing great damage to our nation, besides the obvious problem of bloodshed. It is giving the criminal element the tools of their trade. How do you rob a store without a gun? How do you have a drive by shooting without guns, and so forth? This violence is forcing good people and businesses out of our great cities; driven out by thugs and small time crooks. A war is now in progress between crime and the local and federal law enforcement agencies, which they are beginning to lose. If you don't believe me, go into your city; see how it looks: rundown, crime infested and financially in arrears.

Samuel Colt in 1835 secured patent rights

for a revolving pistol, he had invented while at sea as a boy. His invention revolutionized killing human beings in America. The saying about Colt and his weapon was, "Colonel Colt created all men equal." A person can be as strong as a horse and an expert in the Martial Arts, and it means little going up against another person with a loaded hand gun. Any punk in the inner city can buy a hand gun on the streets for about twenty bucks (due to inflation the price may have gone up), and immediately be in the business of destroying a human life. Any fool can kill the President of the United States with a legally purchased rifle. A single shot in a matter of seconds can destroy a human life, which took a lifetime to build. All it cost is a few bucks.

I haven't said enough about the National Rifle Association. But before I do, my curiosity begs the question about their name, which to me is incomplete; shouldn't it be, The Nation Rifle, Hand Gun and Automatic Weapons Association? Their name sounds rather sporty, when the organization isn't. In order to clear that up, let me tell you what they are. The group's mandate is, all citizens of the USA should be able to purchase and carry guns of all design unhampered by any rules or regulations. Their lobby in Washington scarcely represents .04% of our country's total population, but is one of the best funded organizations of its' kind, influencing members of the US Congress and the office of the President. The NRA's financial might and influence can and has been a factor in winning close federal and local elections. Using this leverage to influence the ruling body of this nation is an awesome power, and it is given to them by money. It touches every citizen in our country. Consider this, free access to guns affects our safety on the streets, increasing the crime rate, thereby adding a tax burden for additional police protection. It closes down businesses in the inner city, which fail due to robberies by gun bearing thieves. Often overlooked are the poor people in this area, who have to travel long distances to buy groceries and other necessities, as a result. One million members of the NRA control over 273 million citizens concerning their survival and everyday life style. Who elected them to this power? I already told you: money.

Yes it is money, but perhaps I'm being unfair in blaming money alone. Perhaps, as I intimated before, it could be argued that money can't do anything without people's general acceptance of the money's message. People believe in money, and bend their knees every day in reverence to it, treating it like a god. The fact is, we in this nation still have a democracy, and can vote out of power any official, who isn't willing to take a stand against the lobbyists' powers. The rub is, we don't. Instead the average citizen respects and even admires violence, and the powers, who represent it. (5) As evidence of this allow me to list the various brutal American heros who have been documented in novels, movies and television narratives.

1. Alphonse (Al) Capone (1899 to 1947) – American gangster and murderer. His crime syndicate terrorized Chicago in the 1920's, controlling gambling and prostitution. In 1931 he was sentenced to prison for federal income tax evasion.

2. Jesse Woodson James (1847 to 1882) – American outlaw and murderer. From 1866 to his death in 1882 he and his brother Frank headed

a band of outlaws, who were responsible for robberies and murders throughout the central United States. He was gunned down by two members of his gang, who betrayed him for the $10,000 reward posted.

     3. Wyatt Earp – (1848 to 1929) – He was a lawman and gunfighter in the American west. After serving as a lawman in Kansas, Earp was involved in the bloodbath gunfight at OK Corral, Tombstone, Arizona.

     4. George Armstrong Custer – (1839 to 1876) – U. S Army Cavalry Officer. He was known for his brutal treatment of the American Indians, which often included mass murders of entire villages (men, women and children). In retaliation he and his entire detachment (7th Cavalry) of 200 men were annihilated by the Sioux and Cheyenne Indians at Little Bighorn, Montana.

     (5) Points 1, 2, 3, 4, 7 source: The Concise Columbia Encyclopedia, Second Edition

     5. (6) Bonnie Parker (1910 – 1934) and Clyde Barrow (1909 – 1934) – well known outlaws, robbers and criminals, who with their gang were notorious for their bank robberies. The gang was believed to have killed at least nine police

officers and committed several other murders.

(6)Source: Bonnie and Clyde – Wikipedia, the free encyclopedia 9/26/09

6. (7) Butch Cassidy and the Sundance Kid – Butch Cassidy (real name Robert Le Roy Parker) 1866 to 1908 teamed up with the Sundance Kid (real name Harry Alonzo Longabaugh) when the latter was released from a Sundance, Wyoming prison for stealing a horse. Their criminal specialties were robbing banks and trains. Robbing the payrolls of the Rocky Mountain West mining company put them on America's most wanted list. The police put a bounty on their heads of $3,000 dead or alive, forcing them to leave the country for refuge in South America. They claimed they never stole from the poor only rich companies, and never hurt anyone only in self-defense. Robbing a payroll – isn't that money earmarked for ordinary people, who have families, children and debt? Isn't that stealing from the poor? Whom did they hurt in self-defense: law enforcement officers? The two were shot to death by a cavalry unit of the Bolivian Army, November 7, 1908 in San Vicente, Bolivia.

(7) Source: this Ring Surf Old West Net

ring, owned by Butch and Sundance in Bolivia, 9/26/09

7. Billy the Kid (1859 to 1881) – was an American outlaw and murderer and large scale cattle rustler in Lincoln Co., N. M. From 1878 he was hunted and fatally shot by Sheriff Pat Garrett. Billy's real name was William H. Bonney.

Abortion, or what is commonly referred to by certain woman's rights groups, as a woman's right of choice, is a good example of money over morality. After all, it costs money to have a baby. From the outset raising a child is not only expensive, but takes up a parent's time and energy, and could interfere with a commitment to a career. It is easier for a pregnant woman to simply go to a free abortion clinic, and have her baby destroyed, no questions asked. This in my opinion is a pathetic decision for anyone to make. However, it has been made millions of times in the United States, proving that money and career are more important to these women than their babies. Money is what drives these people, not morality. Argue all you want about it, and there is a lot of that going on, but at least accept the truth of the matter, which is the taking of a human life. Look at it this way, to hide behind a 'choice' word makes the act more immoral than it is, because you are lying about what it really is, which is a double wrong.

I don't want to make this paper a debating ground for the pro-choice versus pro-life people. All this is getting nowhere for both sides. The fact of the matter is the act was put into law by the Roe versus Wade court decision, which makes it legal and that's that.

I can understand how hard it is to raise a child. I've done that four times. They have all sorts of problems, which fall on the parent's shoulders: illnesses, school difficulties, differences with other children, attention deficits, physical and mental abnormalities and even extreme violence in their nature. Nobody said that following the moral path of parenthood would be easy. It is simpler to go the immoral route of abortion, and lower the world's population. Who needs another hungry child to feed, is another argument for killing them. Yes, there are a great many hungry children in this world, which is a topic for another paper and perhaps a book. I would go along with this debate, if it weren't for the one part of me, which won't let go: my conscience. Conscience is that little voice in you, which directs people to do what's right. It is an instinct to do the right thing, put there by our Maker, an instinct many try to ignore. Every time I hold a newborn baby in my arms, my little voice tells me clearly, that the tiny package of humanity in my arms is the greatest gift God can give mankind. The voice is relentless. If a woman tries to ignore it, and goes ahead with the abortion, the power behind the voice will destroy her. She will be tormented by her conscience, and will hear her unborn child cry out to her forever, even after she herself dies. The money she has chosen will rot away to nothing long before the agony she will endure, because of her evil decision. Is a dollar bill worth that much?

Just briefly getting back to pro-choice versus pro-life differences on the issue of abortion. These groups are well known, making the news a lot. There is no need for me to give them any more ink than they already have. However, with all their fame, there is one more player in this mix, which most people don't know about. He is the silent player, who keeps out of newspapers and off the television, but is a very key figure in this debate, since he fuels the issue, and makes it the hotbed it is. He is the money interest. He is like glass; you can see right through him, and walk right by him, and never know he's there. He provides the money for the free abortion clinics. This is the player nobody knows, because he wants it that way. You can't go against me, if you don't know, who I am. Consider this, where do all the abortion clinics come from, and who funds them? Couldn't be the federal government, since the President of the United States is against abortion. Maybe he is, but is he against abortion clinics? Evidently he isn't, since he isn't doing anything to put them out of business. Consider this, there aren't any free cancer or AIDS' clinics or any other free medical places to go to in our country, which I know about. Why free abortion clinics anyone can go to and get rid of her unborn baby, no questions asked, even with anonymity for young teens. Don't her parents or the father of the baby have a right to at least know about her decision to have the procedure? Evidently not.

There must be a great deal of power behind this baby killing system, since it can circumvent the rights of parents over an under-aged daughter. The authority must come from high up in our American system, and be funded by some big time money.

I don't know why this is the way it is. I can only logically speculate, and connect the dots, so to speak, in order to come up with a clear picture. In the event of an unwanted pregnancy going to full term, the child will most likely be born to poor people, and wind up on the welfare rolls. This costs the government money, and they will have to raise taxes; taxes which will take money from the money people. Isn't it better for the powers to invest in abortion clinics, and kill the baby before he/she is born? This expense is rather small compared to paying for this child over a lifetime? Then the rich can deduct the expense for the clinics from their taxes.

Now the above is only a scenario, and should be treated as such. In no way is this to be taken in whole as a slight against rich people, even if it is true, since poor women have a mind of their own, and can choose to accept their pregnancy. I'm putting it forth, to illustrate how money is preferred by both rich and poor alike over the morality of protecting the life of an unborn child. Birth and propagating one's species is as basic a drive as any creature can have on our planet for it deals with survival. Yet, money takes precedence over a drive this vital! Should that be taken as normal behavior?

Money in our modern day doesn't serve; instead it is served. Money people ask, how can profits be maximized? They aren't concerned about right or wrong in this hypothesis for their money system finds this irrelevant. They are mainly concerned with how their organization can continue to exist, and what it will take to further this goal. In their minds it is clear, money is omnipotent to corporate strength and survival. Achieving a certain profit margin every year is the company's mandate; not how well they treat their employees, their customers or how well they manage their products in order to avoid environment spoilage and ruin from their waste and improper use. If anybody gets in the way of this ambition, regardless of who they are, the corporation will respond as if they are being attacked. Customers, communities and employees are dealt with as if they are the enemy, instead of equal partners in the business. They deal with them using cunning and deceit, instead of with honesty and fair play.

We have all heard of the great oil spills and landfills misuse i.e. illegal burying of toxic waste. Litigation and clean up expenses are frequently part of doing business for many organizations, which try to circumvent proper disposal procedures. It is almost stupid the way firms respond to this, as if it is business as usual, accepting the fools who led them into these disasters, as if they didn't do anything wrong at all, and doing little to keep such mishaps from re-occurring in the future. The best one can expect from the large firm is that the lawyers get involved, and dictate what can be put into place to avoid future law suits from such disasters. Without the threat of court action, the company wouldn't do a thing, because doing something means looking into the system. Their reasoning is to quiet the scandal down as quickly as possible, and get on with business as usual. Further probing into company business by news reporters and the like could result in uncovering embarrassing practices which high up officials would have trouble explaining. Many of such practices are immoral.

(2) This leads us to what some of these practices were and are. Enron, the country's largest energy trader, filed for bankruptcy in December, 2002 while under federal investigation for hiding debts and misrepresenting earnings. The firm used complicated off-the-balance-sheet partnerships to inflate profits by as much as $600 million. Enron's fall had devastating effects on the economy, and left most of its employees short of retirement funds. In July of 2002 Arthur Andersen, the company's accounting firm and auditor was convicted of destroying Enron-related documents.

The corporate scandals didn't end there, WorldCom, the nation's second-largest telecommunications company, went bankrupt after admitting to doctoring its' books. Tyco, Quest, Global Crossing, ImClone, Adelphia, and others, were placed under investigation for various fraudulent practices and crooked accounting. This was in addition to the many different large businesses, whose CEO's were indulged in personal enrichment schemes which demonstrated their arrogance, greed and a criminal disregard for their employees.　The Bush administration was slow to respond to these scandals.

(2)Source:　Time Almanac 2003

Before moving on, my partner and I would like to observe leadership in America.　From our studies and what is common knowledge, it was obvious to conclude, there is something seriously wrong with American leaders.　They seem adept at rising to the highest point in their fields, but once there, they fail.　It seems they lack morality to the point, where the wrongs of their beliefs inhibit them from leading their organization forward; instead they destroy it.　They can't get past their pettiness and greed, looking at their lives as a worldly endeavor, filling their pockets full of money and running off to the Bahamas or some such hideaway.　There is no tomorrow or a hereafter. They are evolutionists and there is no God.　So, take whatever you can, and have no loyalty to anyone but yourself.　Was this what they learned at Princeton or Yale, or wherever they were educated?　Whatever happened to, "honesty is the best policy?"　If the American Empire is to go forward and lead the world, which is where the country placed themselves to be, immorality won't get them there. You can't lead without trust; lying and cheating are the enemies of trust. It takes higher ideals to lead: honesty, courage, empathy, justice, compassion, love, forgiveness. These absolutes build, and should be the cornerstone of the Empire, if it is to succeed.

What companies want today is to separate themselves from their customers: give them a product or service; take their money and move on. The method they opted to utilize in order to do this, is called Customer Service or more like it, Customer Disservice. If you ever have had any dealings with this system, and you must have, if you ever bought anything, and had a problem with it, then you know what I'm talking about. To reiterate the difficult process, it begins with an '800' call to an answering system, and after many, "if it is this, then you press this button", you wind up with a clerk, who can't speak English well enough for you to understand. After about 15 minutes of telling you a bunch of complicated information, which leaves you essentially where you were before you called, you begin to get frustrated, and you start to show your impatience.

From here your service clerk puts you on hold, and an automated system cuts you off completely. That dial tone in your ear is disgusting and rude. The company realizes this, but since it is saving them money, they don't care. It is indeed saving them money and plenty of it. Consider, if you will, a manager working on a problem versus a low paid clerk in Customer Service; it adds up over the long haul. Since everybody (your competition) is doing it, it must be right. It isn't.

This indifference isn't isolated to the customer alone. It is also practiced against the firm's employees in the form of early retirement. This practice is clearly age discrimination, used to get rid of older employees, who are doing a good job. It is particularly offensive to me, since I was a victim of it. Experiencing it, gives me first- hand knowledge of the scheme, which I can pass on to you. Here is what it does: it stipulates a group of workers in a certain age bracket, usually in their mid to late fifties, are to take a retirement package, regardless whether they want to or not. In return the employee(s) are to sign a separation contract, which allows them a pension (for the rest of their lives), and health care benefits up until their

Medicare Insurance begins at age sixty five. If they refuse to sign, they are given a sum of money (they offered me $10,000) and nothing else. As part of the contract the employee waives his right to sue the company. Since they are receiving a pension, the newly retired employee isn't eligible for Unemployment Compensation. If, in addition to their pension, they received a cash settlement, this will put them in a higher tax bracket, and most of that money will go to the Internal Revenue Service.

A friend of mine, who was also being early retired, hired a lawyer to bring suit against the company, using age discrimination as his Constitutional right, which the firm had violated. After investigating the matter, and speaking with the company's Personnel Director, the attorney gave my friend the following counsel: "don't go ahead with this suit, because you will lose. The judge will award you with your pension, and the company will cancel your health care insurance, since this is a privilege and not part of your contract with them." My friend was swayed with the possibility of losing his health care insurance, and so was I. Clearly I had no legal right to go up against the company I worked loyally for, for so many years.   Beaten, I decided to sign on the dotted line, when my separation papers were presented to me and cut my losses as much, as I could.

Clearly from this example, the courts are on the side of the money interests.   This is an important lesson to learn: the courts will always decide on the side of money.   Poor or middle class people will lose in a court of law, unless the suit is for medical malpractice.   There is a reason for this, because lawyers can make a fast buck with medical law suits, and jurors are sympathetic to these cases.   Since judges are lawyers themselves, it stands to reason that they would want their fellow professionals to get rich, which is what is happening.   As part of the mix, there are the large insurance companies, who charge exorbitant premiums for malpractice insurance.   So all players in the mix get rich, and put the doctors out of business.   Medical doctors aren't much, but when you are sick this is all you have.   Lose them, and we are all in a bad position. When they go, it will be a long time before they will be replaced, or perhaps they never will be.   When I'm sick, a doctor looks real good to me.   I can always say no to a risky procedure, or get a second opinion.

Returning to forced early retirement, I firmly believe it is a form of age discrimination. Thus making the practice not only immoral, but against the written law, of the United States Constitution. My friend's attorney confided this to him, and at the same time warned against pursuing it legally. If his assessment is correct and I have no reason to believe otherwise, then the question, "why," should be raised at this point. Rather naively, I'll ask the question, and hope you won't laugh me to scorn for doing so, since the answer must be obvious. Putting it logically in writing has its' advantages of clarifying the details and thereby providing a method of searching out the truth.

The answer must be on the money side of the issue, since this is the Money Country. Let's take a closer look to see, if this is true. To find money in the Money Country, you should look towards big business. It is there, and this is where early retirement takes place. Large Corporations always want to lower administrative costs because this is a firm's largest expense. Since costs are made up mainly of employee salaries and benefits, the money people go after this segment of their organization to bring about cost reductions. Why older employees? Older worker's wages tend to rise over the years of their employment with the company, as a result of pay raises in order to adjust salaries to inflation and to be competitive in the labor market. These employees become targeted, because of this and the rising insurance expense the firm must pay for their benefits.

I'm not saying or even insinuating that judges are on the take with their verdicts on age discrimination. It is more complex. To me it seems the entire legal system is flawed, and not working, as it should. I'm not sure, why. It just doesn't appear to be on the side of the little guy. You can have all the laws you want, and if they aren't being enforced, then they are worthless. Discrimination laws are there, but on paper only, not in men's hearts.

The problem with corporate leaders is they are rather shallow, non– innovative people, who are unable to fully evaluate a situation and come up with the right decision. They look at the surface of a problem, and in putting together a solution to it, they put their faith in taking the path, which provides the right numbers. They have a quick fix mentality, which seldom has any foresight to it. Therefore, if firing the older worker with the higher salary and replacing him with a younger worker who is paid less, is presented as an answer, he opts to do this. What he doesn't take into consideration is worker productivity over the long haul.

(8) Ken Nogan, Risk Control Consultant at PMA Insurance Group wrote a paper entitled, "Capitalizing on an Aging Workforce," which was the first in a quarterly series by the PMA Companies and is called PMA Insights. Concerning worker productivity, he concluded that as over 55 workers increase in the workplace so does productivity and overall workplace safety. He compared such factors as: worker output, sick time taken, desire to serve the customer, respect for company equipment and overall professionalism. In all these categories the older workers excelled over their younger counterparts. These findings led him to two conclusions: one, older workers are a benefit to an organization, and two, it is an advantage to make work station safety

modifications, which limit injuries commonly sustained by older workers.

Looking over the failures and near failures of many large American companies, and you know who they are, age discrimination may have something to do with this fad mania practiced by the organizations infatuated with youth. This is the other side of age discrimination; it evaluates a person by youth, not for what he/she is capable of doing. It stands to reason, the more experience a worker has, the more knowledge and professionalism he can bring to his work place. Yes these companies are now being run by young people, but who is left to train them?

(8a)Source: Safe Workplace and Safety News: Older Workers Mean Greater Safety and Productivity – 9/19/09

Now the very same country (the Money country), which discriminates against older people will turn to Communist China, and have the nerve to tell them that we in the USA are disturbed by their human rights violations. Rather hypocritical wouldn't you say. What is age discrimination? Doesn't that violate a person's human rights? It violated mine, when it happened to me. The loss of my job put me and my family in serious financial difficulty, because I couldn't find a job at my age. This devastated my wife and I and our two school aged children still living at home. What the company did was unfair; they could have handled it another way. Why not give their seniors a little more time to adjust to the inevitable and perhaps reduce their salaries, and set a longer timetable for the separation. This would give them time to adjust and plan for when their incomes would be substantially reduced to their pension benefits. If I had a couple of years to prepare, it would have made quite a difference. No, I don't feel sorry for myself. I feel sorry them.

Returning to Communist China, shouldn't the USA straighten out our own human rights' violations first before concerning themselves with some other country's wrong doings? I don't want to quickly say "yes", because human rights are a concern to all of us, and the USA is correct in challenging this evil, wherever it takes place. The challenge becomes more creditable and convincing, when the nation it comes from is doing the same soul searching within its' own borders.

The tag, "phony" comes to mind, when this is absent.

As earlier noted, the United States was the last major culture to give-up slavery. Although accomplished and duly put into law, this evil institution remains unsettled to this day, leaving a significant group of our black citizens living as second rate peoples. In addition to this and the aforementioned age discrimination, the U. S. harbors industries, which close their doors to small businesses, aspiring actors and other members of the entertainment business, including writers. It is also well known that women in certain jobs don't earn the same money, as their male counterparts. Unfortunately discrimination is still alive here, and little is being done to turn this around, I'm sorry to report. Now with a history of being troubled by discrimination i.e. the Civil War, street violence in many of our major cities, strikes, protests, general unrest, racial divisions, etc., our nation should have learned discrimination flat out doesn't work. Up until a point, where a great civil rights President (JFK) was shot and killed, we did, and passed a law in his memory stipulating the various types of this bias were unlawful. It is so written in the twenty fourth amendment to the US Constitution, the law of our land. As with a lot of good ideas, the law is being danced around, and my nation is looking for some other way of discriminating, which I believe they have found. The new discrimination fall guys are old people. How bad is this going to get? There has already been a movement in Congress to raise the Social Security and Medicare benefits age to seventy years old for a recipient's eligibility. Between early retirement and this proposed increase in age eligibility, it places the average older person fifteen years without enough money to pay bills and receive Health Care Insurance. Understanding the legislature's thinking on this referendum, one could easily come to the conclusion that they want all us old folks to die off from starvation and disease. Thank God the law wasn't passed, mainly due to public pressure and a caring president, who made it clear to Congress that he would veto such a bill if it came across his desk. This does give you a good idea of how certain American leaders are thinking about our seniors.

The "baby boomers" aren't babies any longer. In time their entry into old age will have a profound effect on the economy and political aspects of the nation. Today old people aren't what they used to be. We are stronger, healthier, more educated and most significantly, we can vote in large numbers. There will come a time, when the powers will shift, and the elderly will have their voice. We won't ask for our rights; we will demand them, through the election polls and our buying strength. The day is coming! Indeed the meek will be inheriting the earth. Let's see how the money interests are going to dance around that fact!

I always loved sports, especially baseball. The game was not only competitive and exciting, but had statistics involved to evaluate it and its' players: Earned Run Average, Runs Batted In, Batting Averages, Won/Loss records, Number of Home Runs, Doubles, Triples, Stolen Bases, etc. As a boy when I had a bad day, I would think of these figures and the players, who were graded by them. It helped me sleep at night. Every day I would study the baseball statistics in the newspaper, and get a broad look at the players represented. The numbers for the most part seemed to give a clear picture of the player's talent and ability to perform, so I could see the entire National and American League just by reading the sport's page. The game was indeed intriguing for me, and in time became my favorite pastime, which lasted a lifetime.

Unfortunately, like all good things which happen in the Money Country, the money interests would make their presence known and edge their way into the control and administration of the sport. Money has literally ruined sports in this country, and in other nations as well, but especially here in America. To give you an example, when I was a boy, it cost $.15 to take the elevated train to Connie Mack Stadium, and $.50 admission to see the Philadelphia A's play ball. Okay, so they didn't win much, but we loved them anyway. They were a fun team to watch; not a lot of talent, but they always did their best, and gave the fans a good show worth the price of admission. Games were colorful with an occasional burst of anger between players and verbal arguments with umpires, a cloud of dust sliding into bases and acrobatic catches in the field. I know we still have these plays today at times, but back then there was more of this action, since players were honest to the sport and less afraid of getting injured.

The A's were always underdogs, especially when they went up against the more talented squads, such as the New York Yankees, Boston Red Sox, Chicago White Sox or the Cleveland Indians. On the other hand they weren't always in last place, the Washington (DC) Senators and the St. Louis Browns shared that position, more often than the A's. No one on the squad made big money, so the ticket prices weren't high. Of course the fans wanted a winner, but that wasn't going to happen, so you became accustomed to what you had, and rooted for them to pull off the sporadic upset, which would act as a spoiler for some good team's quest for a pennant.

It was fun to talk with friends about our local hero little Bobby Shantz shutting out the great New York Yankees. Of course, I was never at Connie Mack when this happened, but my pride was just as strong regardless. Anybody beating the great Yankees was high on our list, since we all hated them because they were so good. The A's didn't have a lot of stars on their team, but many squads in the Junior Circuit did. A day at Mack Stadium for a couple of bucks gave us a chance to see Yogi Berra, Joe DiMaggio, Ted Williams, Bob Feller, George Kell and others. Guess what, the game was played on natural grass.

There were great stars back then on those teams, but they weren't stuck up prima donnas. These athletes played when they were injured; made all the practices, shook your hand, and gave you an autograph regardless of how busy they were. No one took steroids or performance enhancing drugs, went on protesting Union walkouts and strikes, or gambled on the game. They were regular human beings just like you and me. You could identify with them because they identified with you. Most of them had jobs in the off-season; had a family and a mortgage to pay like the average fan. If they were medical doctors, they would have made house calls.

I remember the Philadelphia A's with fondness. They were special to me and still are. I never flipped their baseball card pictures in the game of odds and evens; not wanting to lose any of them. In time like many of life's treasures, I did lose them all to a mother, who believed I had outgrown my collection interests, and gave them to

my younger cousins.   How could you have done
this to me mom?   Oh well, that's the way she
was; always generous with other people's
property.   With all her depletion of my cigar box
card collection, she couldn't give away my
memories.   They remain.   Here are the names
and the positions they played of my favorite
baseball team of all time: the 1951 Philadelphia
A's.

Joe Tipton, Catcher

Ferris Fain, First Baseman

Pete Suder, Second Baseman

Hank Mageski, Third Baseman

Eddie Joost, Shortstop

Gus Zernial, Left Field

Dave Philley, Center Field

Elmer Valo, right Field

Bobby Shantz, Pitcher

Alex Kellner, Pitcher

Jimmy Dykes, Manager

Here I am now, forty five years later,

rooting for the Philadelphia Phillies, who have the same ranking in their respected league as the A's did before they left: about fifteen games under a five hundred won/loss percentage. However, there is one main difference facing me and all baseball fans, and that is money. The ticket prices for seeing a game are sky high; along with that are parking cost, snacks, beer, souvenirs and whatever the stadium vendors can get out of your wallet. Take your kids to a ballgame, and you can easily drop several hundred dollars in an afternoon. It almost makes me glad that my kids are all grown up. They're not interested in seeing a ball game with Dad any longer.

I can't tell you who is on the Phillies' team, because they change almost every year. They do keep a few good players like the third baseman, who wins the gold glove every year, and can hit the long ball. I can't remember his name, which is no big deal, because the team will probably trade him in a year or two to a contender. Along with him is that all-star catcher, what's-his-name; he's good too. I guess you need to have some quality players, or nobody will go see the team play. How can the team advertise, if they don't have a drawing card?   Wouldn't it look ludicrous to have a spread in the newspapers with the picture of a journeyman player and a triple "A" prospect from the Reading Phillies on it?   It wouldn't sell many tickets, would it?   The team has to pay the multi-million dollar contracts to the hot shot third baseman and the all-star catcher, What's-his-name.   When am I ever going to remember these guys' names?

   I don't go to baseball games anymore; they are starting to bore me.   Perhaps I've experienced too many losing seasons here in Philadelphia with the also ran Phillies.   It is more than just losing, which bothers me with them.   They seem to be content with defeat.   I can almost predict the outcome of the losing games.   They go something like this: the team gets behind by a couple of runs; they give up, and become more lethargic, roll over and die, then walk off the field with heads down.   The franchise appears to have a give-up philosophy, which permeates the entire organization from the ownership on down through every section of the team, especially the players. This is the type product the organization puts on the field every year.   At best they are looking for a

500 percentage won/loss squad at the end of the season, and usually they don't get that much. The type players they employ are content to play out the game regardless of whether they win or not, then take their paycheck at the end of the week and run with it. They have very little affinity towards the city or the fans, and the organization has little affinity towards them. The team pretends to give them an opportunity and career here, and they pretend to play good baseball. However, in the back of their minds they know the truth, and I believe the fans know it too.

Unfortunately there are a good many teams in the major leagues, who have this attitude, so I'm not just picking on the Phillies alone. At the other end of the spectrum are the Yankees and the other big time franchises, who spend large sums of money in the free agency market and buy a championship. This isn't always the case, but the exception is indeed rare in the sport. The norm is evident that both organization types are money driven, one way or the other. The outcome is a product, which is boring and somewhat predictable. This is baseball, and with all its faults, and regardless of what I think, the game remains popular.

What bothered me recently was an interview on television given by one of our local reporters and the Phillies all-star catcher, what's-his-name. He was complaining about the then current stadium, and felt the city should build a new stadium with real grass and state-of-the-arts niceties, where someone of his all-star capabilities could play out his wonderful career. It sounded as if he wanted it ready made for him. His comments appeared arrogant to me. His job is to catch and get hits, which belonged on the field. He wasn't running the front office, and his opinions on a new stadium were out of line. What I wanted out of him was, comments concerning playing the game, and what he was going to do to make the Phillies a better team on the field. Instead here he is inactive, nursing an injury, and running his mouth about something, which wasn't any of his business, and making millions while doing it. "Nice work if you can get it," as the saying goes.

Note: This catcher is no longer playing major league ball.

Joe Tipton didn't care where he played; just

as long as he played. He and his teammates all took the field with injuries at one time or another. A player healed in the off-season; that's what this time is for, for chrissake! If some stupid reporter asked him about a new stadium, he probably would have laughed his ass off, and spit some tobacco juice on the man's shoe. So Joe was a little rough around the edges. All he was supposed to do was catch, and handle a rag-tag pitching staff (Bobby Shantz not included). He was satisfied to do this every game, and play his heart out for his fans. This was the real difference between the old A's and the new Phillies. Sure they were both losers, but the A's were exciting to watch, because they hated losing and fought the entire game to win. The Phillies are just as talentless, but accept their plight meekly, and walk off the field after a loss, looking like losers. The A's never looked like losers, and their fans appreciated their determination and swagger. Unfortunately, they didn't appreciate it enough, because we lost the team to Kansas City and then to Oakland. I was heartbroken! Philadelphia lost its' best franchise by the numbers. Up until the year 2001, the A's made fourteen World Series appearances winning nine and losing five; The Phillies: five appearances, winning one and losing four. The Phillies are the only franchise in the history of major league baseball, who lost over 10,000 games.

The Phillies and the old A's comparison for me, illustrates where the sport has gone in the past fifty years. Sports in general, including baseball, have gotten very commercial and money centered, more of a business than a competitive sport. There's a difference between the two: in a sport an athlete plays for the love of the game and the competition of winning. In a business the athlete plays for the love of money. I played basketball competitively on and off for many years, and during that time I never earned a nickel doing it. I did make many friends through the game. We tortured our bodies, and took on countless injuries, because we all loved the sport and the desire to win, it evoked in us. In the NBA the players are losing the game part of the sport, so essentially it is more business than sport. When a player is out on the court making ten million dollars a year, you can't call this a game anymore. It is now a big time business, and the players are beginning to treat it this way. If they get the slightest injury, they immediately stop playing, lay down on the floor/ground and await trainer(s) to attend to them like they are some sort of China doll. They are gently carried off the field to be examined by a team doctor, ex-rays taken at the site, and then rushed to a specialty hospital, which specializes in that particular medicine. If necessary, surgery is scheduled for the next day. This is 'big wheel' treatment!

When the regular season is over, most well-known sports figures don't get a performance evaluation, as most of us do. Instead, they have an expensive agent negotiate or renegotiate their contract. This at times can go on for a lengthy time, keeping the athlete from joining the team. None of us normal working types can do this; if we spend any time away from our jobs, we will certainly lose them.

Note: Allow me at this time to apologize to the Philadelphia Phillies organization for most of my derogatory comments. This paper was written, when they had a mediocre team. This in recent years has changed; almost a complete turnaround. The team has won three division titles, and one world championship. We in Philadelphia are indeed proud of their accomplishments. By the way, they do have a new state-of-the-arts stadium, with a real grass playing diamond.

Probably the worse voting scandal, I can recall, happened in the 2000 Gore/Bush presidential election. If it didn't destroy my belief in the American system of democracy, it came pretty close to it. The scandal centered on a possible miscount of votes in the state of Florida, which was so vital to the outcome of that state's part in this close national election, that their electoral votes, given to either candidate would carry the election accordingly. The Gore camp decided to challenge the count legally, citing several questionable activities, which were brought to their attention concerning the methods used in counting the votes, and the voters' access to physically reaching the voting polls. Expeditiously, the case moved up the legal system, until it reached the United States Supreme Court. This body, trying to duck responsibility in deciding the issue, returned the case to the Florida Supreme Court, who favored a recount. Upon hearing this, the US Court retracted their own decision, and retried the case, they didn't want to try. Their verdict was against a vote recount, which essentially gave the electoral votes and the election to George W. Bush. The US Supreme Court's reasons behind their judgment were so vague and illogical that the paper written on the majority view, sounded like utter nonsense. The writer of the majority view blew so much smoke at the American public, it was difficult for the average person to understand what she was talking about, let alone the legality behind the verdict. However, the result of all that smoke was quite clear. The highest court in the land stopped the recount of some twenty thousand plus votes, which could have changed the outcome of the Florida's part in the presidential election. To repeat what I stated earlier, their ruling gave the Presidency of the United States of America to George W. Bush, who just happened to be of the same party affiliation as five of the nine members of the court, who just happened to have voted en masse against the recount. Of course this just happened that way, since the Court should be above party affiliation and politics. I'm not through with, "just happenings:" the state of Florida just happened to have George W.'s brother Jeb Bush as their governor, who just happened to have promised his brother the state of Florida electoral votes, no matter what he had to do to get it for him. Now I'm not saying that Jeb did anything illegal because there is no proof of this for the investigation and recount weren't allowed. For me, there were so many "just happenings" going on in this election that I just happened to smell a rat. Now there are some, who would argue that these "just happenings", just happened the way they did. Or worse still, say questionable events do have a way of showing up in elections, and the country has a history of this voter deceit. Just shake it off, as nothing more than that. Shame on you, if you think this way. You are far worse than the naive "just happening" fools, because you know better. Voter deceit is wrong and should be seriously dealt with by the courts. Without voter trust, we have nothing; certainly not a democracy.

Like the John F. Kennedy assassination, all the involved leadership will attempt to cover this scandal up, because they are afraid of the big bad dog, the American people, will rise up and bite them, and so they should be. Americans quiet the scandal down as quickly as possible, and return to business as usual. Lie to the dog; that will quiet him down; that always works. But does it? The dog isn't that stupid. He knows when he is being lied to by his leaders. He returns to business as usual, because this is all he has. He doesn't forget. The scandal will have an effect on his thinking and it does, whether the leadership understands this or not. Investors, who are the backbone of the American economy, react to scandals in government. Cover-ups don't fool them. They respond accordingly, and begin to put their money in safe investments, which is a tendency away from common stock. The investment in common stock has long been an indicator of the success of the American economy. Investments make this country move and grow. When they slow down, so does the economy, jobs, tax base, etc. It is a downward spiral, which is difficult to reverse.

(9)To illustrate my point allow me to list the Dow Jones year ending closing averages, during G. Walker Bush's Presidency.

2000 (Clinton administration) climbed 65.60 points

2001 (Bush administration) climbed 5.68 points

2002 (Bush administration) climbed 29.07 points

2003 (Bush administration) climbed 125.33 points

2004 (Bush administration) declined 25.35 points

2005 (Bush administration) declined 67.32 points

2006 (Bush administration) declined 38.37 points

2007 (Bush administration) climbed 6.26 points

2008 (Bush administration) climbed 184.46 points

As with all statistics, these averages are open for interpretation. My interpretation is there is a direct correlation between the two times Mr. Bush was elected to office and the reaction of the market. Both of his elections were marred with suggestions of voting scandal i.e. 2000 election – Florida; 2004 election – Ohio. The American voter will never know the truth of these scandals, since the proper investigations were never authorized. Of course, I don't want to neglect the obvious: the man's poor performance in office also reflected these averages. His two terms were culminated with a total collapse of the nation's economy. We all paid dearly for Mr. Bush's fraudulent practices in getting elected, and ineptness in running the country i.e. losing our homes, our jobs, our financial security, and God knows what more.

(9)Source: The Dow Jones statistics –
New York Times Company End of Year Quotes,
Copyrighted by the New York Times each year,
Delaware County Library System.

Perhaps honesty is the best policy!   It is an
intangible; not like money, but it has power, since it
lasts a long time.   Money dies and rots away, but
honesty is strong and lasting.   It breeds trust and
integrity.   May I suggest honesty is better than
money?   G. Walker Bush built his Presidency on
dishonesty and money.   Where did it get him and
the country?   I'm not going to respond to that
question, since history has already done so for me,
and you the taxpayers are well aware of the
outcome.   Everything my partner and I wrote about
here, is a plea that our country will one day temper
its' desire for money with the wealth and wisdom
of honesty.

End of THE MONEY COUNTRY

THE PLEDGE

When I was a boy in parochial school, I was selected to lead the class in reciting the Pledge of Allegiance every morning. I never minded doing it; it was short and to the point and easy to memorize. The words were stirring and patriotic sounding, making me feel fortunate to be an American, living in this great land of ours. The recitation was spoken freely with Old Glory held as high as my little seven year old hands could raise her.

The manifesto probably hasn't changed at all over the years. My recollection of it went something like this:

"I pledge Allegiance to the flag of the United States of America and to the Republic for which it stands, one nation under God, indivisible, with Liberty and Justice for all."

(10)Note: The original pledge was published in the September 8, 1892 issue of The Youth's Companion in Boston, MA, credited to Francis Bellamy of the magazine's staff. The phrase "under God" was added to the pledge on June 14, 1954.

Back then the words came out of me with little thought about what they truly meant. They sounded patriotic, and since there was a strong post Second World War nationalistic fervor during this period, my rationale was to totally agree with their meaning, and not to evaluate or question their validity. As with every great piece of writing, The Pledge has survived the test of time, and is still with us today, as it was in my youth. What brought it to my attention recently, was the controversy concerning the use of "under God," being a part of it. As a result I reviewed the sentence, and came up with many questions concerning its truth, which I must state isn't the fault of the author, but lies as a fault of the American system, the least of which is the reference to God. I would like to review these words, and see how they stack up today. The inspiring words are: allegiance, republic, nation under God, liberty, justice, for all. My eyes look at them with more questions now than they did in my youth. Could I recite these stirring words again in front of a group with the same unshaken belief as in my boyhood? Have the institutions and traditions which brace our democracy, lived up to their commitment of opportunity and fair play for all? Have we as a nation respected and supported the civil liberties of our citizens? Has our democracy survived, or has it lapsed into a 'big brother' type dictatorship, controlled by the money interests? The answers given as a result of my research are as perplexing as the questions themselves, and shouldn't be, since our rights and liberties are God given, and provided for by the founding fathers in words all of us can understand.

I'll try to be objective about my evaluation, even if the only changes I find are in me, and not in the fulfillment of the country's promises. Let me begin with ALLEGIANCE. This is the average citizen's side of the Pledge. It asks, what is my responsibility to my nation? Have I served in the military, paid my taxes honestly, been a good neighbor, obeyed the laws, etc. Yes, is my answer to all of these questions. Did I teach my children to do the same? Yes. Did I vote? Yes, I did, even when the candidates weren't qualified for the posts, and my beliefs were beginning to dwindle in the two party system. The doubts grew in me over the years, and the disappointments became realities too apparent to ignore. Even a greater let down, was the fact that my fellow citizens were giving up on the voting system because they too could see the problems seeping into it, and were losing any fervor they originally possessed. Along with this, they would disobey minor laws if they felt they could get away with it. Cheating on their income taxes was commonplace. The people didn't challenge the system in court, looking on it as a rich person's toy, which is what it became. Police were viewed as the enemy; a group who abused the electorate along with the criminals. In a democracy, this isn't a good mind-set for the people, who are responsible for their own government. This slowly evolved into a trend. Allegiance was just another fancy word; not an obligation.

REPUBLIC – is a government for and by the people, which is what the founding fathers created, when they designed our country. Has their creation survived the test of time? It is easy enough to find out. Try writing to a judge challenging her verdict; try writing your congressman or the president about a problem;

and see what you get back as an answer, if you get an answer at all. I wrote several letters to the then president, G. Walker Bush, and received no reply, not even a form letter. I read somewhere that the man doesn't read anything. Can that be true? I did receive back form letters from the judge and congressman, but no satisfaction. It was as if there was no communication at all, only a passing of letters back and forth, which were meaningless.

I had two friends of mine, who belonged to a group who picketed the abortion clinics, which is their right under the law. They were in jail more than they were out, subjected to every demeaning and cruel punishment the police could dole out such as extra tight hand cuffs, which cut into their wrists, strip searches, with rubber gloves and the like. They told me they expected this sort of treatment; it was what the police did. How are the police serving and protecting the public doing this? My friends weren't criminals; they were simply testing the system; getting involved, which is their right, the right to assembly.

I was in the nation's capital, visiting. Early one morning I decided to take a walk around the area where all the government buildings were located. In time nature began to call. Passing a government building, I decided to enter it, and use their restroom. At the entrance hall a guard, who couldn't speak English well, rudely asked me for identification. I told him what I was there for, but he still insisted. Showing him my driver's license, he refused to return it. I told him it was my property; he still refused. Reaching over I grabbed hold of his arm and tore the card out of his hand. Like a corrected child, he threatened to call the police, which he did. I decided to wait outside for them to see, if they came. A car did pass by, but not for me; it was just a cop making his rounds. I waited longer, until my bladder was about to burst. Guess where I relieved myself; the building had a very lovely garden out front. You know the old saying: when you have to go, you have to go. The point I'm trying to make is, I am a taxpayer and entitled to enter a public building, if I want. No one has a right to take what belongs to me and detain me.

One more comment about police brutality. Many Americans look on it as something, which comes with the territory of being a cop, since police deal with hardened criminals, and must respond in kind. These naïve citizens go along with this, because in the isolation of their little lives, they believe such treatment won't happen to them. But it could; no one is immune to this treatment, especially if it is tolerated. It is happening more in this country than most of us realize. In a republic, such violence from law enforcement officers has no place. The police in this form of government are required to enforce the law and serve the public; not to go around beating the crap out of them. The overzealous cops, who practice this sort of treatment are seldom reprimanded, since the police take care of their own. This is a major reason, why police in general are becoming more ineffective, not only in the performance of their duty, but in gaining the trust of the very people they are supposed to serve.

In all fairness to the police, it should be noted that the court system, they are working under, is overly lenient and protective toward lawbreakers. This doesn't excuse police brutality, but one can see how frustrating and difficult it is for them under such restraints. The courts in order to keep the police under control are essentially punishing the American public in doing so, resulting in allowing hardened criminals to escape the punishment they deserve, due to technicalities. When brought to trial, extreme care must be exercised that the accused person's rights be explained to them, or the case can be thrown out of court. Additionally, key evidence can be withheld from the case as a result of an illegal search, or some such detail, which was overlooked in the investigation. Essentially the American public is receiving bad police work compounded by a bad court system.

The challenge I'm putting forth here is: one, why don't the courts and the police have a better working relationship, designed to further the interests of the American public? Two, why aren't the victims of crimes given equal treatment under the law? Nobody in the system reads the victim his rights, nor notifies him of the possible outcome of the court's decision. Many times the victim and his family are quite surprised by the law and the decision rendered under it. Isn't there a problem with justice here?

(2) Congress in 1862, in order to fund the

Civil War effort, enacted the nation's first income tax law. It was the model of our modern income tax system in that it was based on the principles of graduated, or progressive, taxation and of withholding income at the source. The Act established the office of Commissioner of Internal Revenue. This official was given the power to assess, levy, and collect taxes, and the right to enforce the tax laws through seizure of property, income, as well as through prosecution. His powers and authority remain very much intact today.

(2)Source: TIME Almanac 2003, Page 1019 .

Wars come and go, but tax laws remain. Let me repeat the important part of the Act which refers to the American citizen, "the IRS has the power to assess, levy, and collect taxes, and the right to enforce the tax laws through seizure of property and income and through prosecution." In short they can offset your human rights under the United States Constitution. Have you ever been audited by the IRS? It is a harrowing experience, where they can go back five years into your tax filing, and fine you for anything they feel is out of line. It is their decision; they have the power and final ruling on the matter. You better pay up or you stand to lose your home and assets or go to jail. As a result most Americans are so frightened of having any dealings with the IRS bureaucracy, they go to professional accountants and hire them to file their yearly tax claim. The accountant's bill is like getting an additional tax. The accountant does one more important job: he is there to understand the government's Income Tax Form. The IRS just can't tax you; they want to annoy the hell out of you too with a yearly income tax filing document which is difficult for the average tax payer to read and process. The tax form is so complicated that the IRS themselves can't understand it. Many times I've discussed taxing provisions over the phone only to receive incorrect information on the matter from IRS customer service representatives. So you can see why accounting firms are in business, and go so far as to assure you, they will go with you to the IRS, if audited.

Can't this IRS bullying system of taxation be improved? In Pennsylvania we have a simple income tax system: if you (the resident) make X number of dollars, you pay Y number of taxes. It takes about five minutes to make out the tax filing paperwork, and return it to Harrisburg. It seems to work for them!

Welfare is also a part of our republic. The program gives money and food stamps to those, who have no source of income, and are forced to go to the state in order to receive assistance until such time, when they can get back on their feet again. The problem with the US system is, it doesn't ask the recipients to work for the money they receive, nor does it provide a strategy of finding jobs for them. Granted welfare is needed, but isn't there a better way of administering it? I can't help but notice that the streets, where welfare people live are filthy dirty, littered with trash, graffiti covered walls, and the like. It is a bad sign; it tells me something is desperately wrong, and change must come about or the people involved in it will deteriorate even more. The thought crosses my mind: is it asking too much for welfare people to form cleanup crews, and collect the trash for proper disposal in order to earn their welfare checks? Or perhaps, they should fix up the properties they live in, and put a coat of paint on the place every now and then. Surely the government would agree to provide the supplies and tools needed for such endeavors. Of course I'm referring to able bodied people to perform this work. Those who are unable to work such as the disabled, sickly and bedridden would be excused, with a doctor's note. As an adjunct to this, older people on welfare can be put to work, running day care centers for moms to go out and look for employment, and perform their duty to the neighborhood. To administer such a program, it may work to hire people who are on welfare, since they are closest to the problem, and are best qualified to deal with it. Quarterly, semiannual and yearly audits and inspections can be scheduled to supervise each welfare group sections.

My belief is the folks on welfare are desperate to get off it, because it is so demoralizing and hopeless. Give the welfare people a system for escaping their dilemma, and I believe they will respond to it in a positive way. I know because I walked a mile in their shoes. I was on relief, when I was a young man. Believe me, it is far better to work than to sit around all day, and go bad.

ONE NATION UNDER GOD – There is a movement in the United States to remove God from every institution we have in this wonderful land of ours, using the "separation of church and state" clause in the Constitution as the legal basis for such an action. To review the movement's position and reflect on it, the Constitution doesn't say, "separation of God and state," nor does it say, "separation of church and state," for that matter. What it does say is, "Congress shall make no law respecting an establishment of religion..., and as far as I know the Congress hasn't. Also, God isn't the Church; He is above that, and as such He is above all things material or mental. If you are an atheist with money, it is enough to twist this provision around to force your views on an entire nation founded on religious freedom, also provided for in the Constitution. What I don't understand is, why this has become an issue in the first place. How does saying a prayer in the public school threaten the country or its' citizens? Nothing my partner and I read or researched can answer this question. We can show you how it all got started, however.

On June 17, 1963 the Supreme Court ruled (8 to 1), laws requiring recitation of the Lord's Prayer or Bible verses in public schools were unconstitutional. This ruling opened up the flood gates to every quack, who hates God. Okay, they don't hate God; they simply believe, He doesn't exist, and are offended by all the billions of people in the world, who believe He does. We offer this explanation of their stand on the matter, and of course we accept this as their right of opinion. Will it end there? This doesn't explain the Supreme Court's ruling on the dispute. We are of the opinion that the Court has stepped out of line in this ruling, and feel strongly that their verdict is illegal, since it isn't in the scope of the federal, but is interfering with a local issue. As such, it is the business of the various school boards, since they are best qualified to determine what should be taught in their schools.

Freedom of Religion isn't just three little words. The concept is a challenge to the country, which espouses it and puts it into law. When the Declaration of Independence, which was adopted by the Continental Congress on July 4, 1776, and unanimously endorsed by all thirteen United States of America, was written, it became that challenge. To have the highest court in the land say the country no longer has that challenge is upsetting and illogical. As long as The Declaration is still respected and held as the nation's written policy, we, including The Court must respect it and pass no laws, which go against it. This is what the document states from its' second paragraph, "We hold these truths to be self-evident that all men are created equal, that they are endowed by their CREATOR with certain inalienable rights, that among these are life, liberty and the pursuit of happiness."

My partner and I both agree, we have the God given right to enter into any public building, which our tax money is paying for, and pray, openly, if we feel like it. We also believe our schools, which our tax money pays for, should be free to explore the existence of God and teach their students about Him, if they so choose. These are our basic freedoms provided for by the founding fathers of this great nation of ours, and put into writing in the US Constitution.

I will personally end this by reflecting sadly,

that when I was a boy reciting the Pledge of Allegiance to the Flag in front of my class, I never thought "God" would ever be taken out of the schools, and the highest court in the land would even consider making such a ruling. However, it is done, and we all have to live with it. One more right, taken away from the American public.

(1)Source: The World Almanac and Books of Facts 1999, Page 521

LIBERTY – Does every American have equal opportunity to succeed in our country? Will we ever have an Abraham Lincoln, who began as a rail splitter, and wound up president of the United States with his picture on the five dollar bill? It is unlikely that this will ever happen again, because more and more monopolistic structures are in place, which limit opportunity to the everyday person. It is hard to break through this power base, and get your foot in the door, so to speak.

Granted, I maybe setting my goal too high using the US presidency as an example. Perhaps a lower post(s) would be more realistic, since not everyone can achieve this position. How about a congressman, a CEO in a large corporation, a sports star, an industrialist, a prima ballerina, a writer – successfully published, an inventor, a doctor, a lawyer? Okay, not everyone can be a big wheel. Can the average Joe do better than just getting by? Do we have hard working poor in this country of vast wealth? Are poor people poor because they are too lazy to go out and get a job? Can the normal father support his family on his income alone? Is there opportunity left in this "land of opportunity," or has the opportunity been snatched up by opportunists? Can you have a dream and have it fulfilled? Are there prejudices in this country, which are allowed to exist robbing good people of their liberty? Can one speak his or her mind freely without coming under scrutiny from politically correct do–gooders, who actually don't believe in correcting anything? Let me pause for a moment from my "can we" listings to go over the political corrective nonsense.

I'll call it PC. What does PC do for poor people, assuming the concept is aimed at the less fortunate? Does it put food on their dinner tables, get them better housing, better education, jobs, health care insurance? I don't believe it does. It simply provides a name to call these people, and blows smoke at them, so they won't complain about their situation. (NB: This statement is not and I repeat not excusing the n____ word! It is indeed offensive and insulting.) With all that said, let's get back to the "can we" listings.

Can we walk the streets safely at night? Do we have adequate police protection in all neighborhoods? Can we get a quality job, if we are over sixty years old? Does the average tax payer get a good return on his tax investment? Is his money being spent for beneficial programs, which directly enhance his life style? Is an across the board tax cut going more to the average tax payer or to the wealthy? Does the citizen's vote count, or is there election fraud?

I've asked a lot of questions, and gave no answers, but the fact that the questions exist implies the problems they represent also exist. Consequently, they must be asked by the citizen and put forth as issues. In a republic the rights of the populace must be communicated to the government representatives and settled to make the system work. Liberty isn't just a word on some coins. It is an obligation, and a precious gift given to us by our founding fathers. Do we still have it in this land of ours?   Only if we want it.

JUSTICE – Have you been involved in a civil or criminal court case recently?   It is a worthwhile experience, if you want to get an understanding of your country's idea of justice. The procedures and methods used will surprise you.   They did me, when I was involved in it.

Up until about five years ago, my experience with the courts was with summons to jury duty, which always ended in me not being selected on a case.   My background in the legal system was limited to this one day visit to the court house, which occurred every two to four years, or whenever the court house computer spit out my name.   This shelter from the legal reality would end, when I was asked to appear as a witness in a felony criminal case.   Not only was I a witness, but the victim as well.   The township police were pressing charges, so they thought they had a solid case against the suspect.   The magistrate agreed with the police at the hearing, and bound the case over to the county court.   A date was set for the trial to begin in two months.

At this point the victim gets a taste of what

American justice is all about. It's as ugly as the crime itself and the person, who perpetrated it. From here I want to cut to the chase, and not get too involved in the crime itself. Briefly, I was assaulted by another neighbor, who had recently moved in down the block, where I lived. It happened on my driveway. I was sixty years old at the time, and he was half that age. The attack began with my assailant jumping me from behind, and driving my face into a group of brambles on the property. From this advantage he was able to land several punches, which aggravated the cuts on my face. Fortunately, the gashes were mostly superficial, but one penetrated deeply just under my right eye, enough to cut an artery in my face, which in turn caused heavy bleeding during the assault. According to police procedure, I had to be taken to a nearby hospital to confirm my injuries. A few stitches by an intern there, stopped the bleeding of the deep cut, and I was released.

Now you would think with a felony trial pending, the victim would get police protection. Not so, the attacker came up to my house every day trying to goad me into a fist fight. The police did nothing about it, but promised to talk to the defendant's lawyer, who did nothing about it.

As a matter of fact he advised his client to do the goading. When discussing this problem with my lawyer, he told me this was standard procedure in such a case. That my giving in to this, and getting into another fight, could be used against me in the upcoming case. He advised I should go into my house, when it happens and do nothing. He did sympathize with me, and agreed I was giving up my civil liberties in doing so, but it would only be temporary, until the case was over.

Note: While all this was going on, the defense attorney contacted the Personnel Department, where I worked, and explained the upcoming assault case. He asked, if I had any problems with losing my temper and any situations of violence with other employees. I was once more being placed in a position of having to defend myself for doing my duty in a court of law. I wonder, if the prosecuting attorney contacted the place, where the accused worked?

Getting back to the goading, I did what my attorney suggested, and the trial date finally came. My thinking was that this would end the problem. I believed my attacker would be convicted, and either sent to jail, or be put on probation, then I could get on with my life. Wrong! In a bench trial, the judge found him, not guilty. A bench trial is tried by a judge only – no jury. I had no say in this selection; the defendant did. In fact no one told me about it, until the day of the trial. One person decided the case; she went against the police detective's testimony, who investigated the case, and overwhelming amounts of evidence presented to her, and also my testimony as a witness, as well. I guess victims aren't considered trustworthy in the legal system.

If my life was hell up until then, it really got bad after the trial. The man came up the street to my house several times a day, insulting me, threatening me, and just being a pain in the ass in general. He later told me, he was going to sue me for wrongful arrest. Probably his lawyer encouraged him to do this. What his attorney forgot to tell him was that the police pressed charges against him, not me. I was only a witness. Who knows, maybe an arrested felon can sue a witness today, and I just don't know about it.

At this time, I wrote a letter to the judge,

whose verdict put me in this dilemma, and explained everything which was going on since the trial. Much to my surprise, she did answer my letter. It was a form letter, but it was better than nothing. Her reply was, she followed adjudicative procedures in trying the case, and that I should notify the police, and they would instruct me how my problem could be worked out in a court of law.

Well, the whole deal was starting to look like a "passing the buck" routine to me, but regardless, I had nowhere else to go, so the police were my next step. A patrolman came after my first complaint. His advice, according to the law, was for me to keep a log on the number of times my assailant threatened me. Over a period of time, I could use this in a court of law, and have charges brought against my stalker for harassment. I did this for a couple of months, calling the police periodically as a situation arose, to go on record with them. At about this time my patience was starting to wear thin. This coupled with a visit from a nasty cop with an attitude, who answered one of my calls, brought out something negative in me. He intimated that I was harassing the harasser. I told that SOB off, before asking him to leave. He seemed quite shaken by my outburst. That didn't placate me, nor did the bad feeling which was growing in me, concerning the legal system, and my ability to work within it. I decided to take care of the problem myself. I went on record with the police, the judge and anybody else, who would listen to me that I was going to kill the stalker. I didn't have long to wait for an opportunity; a few days later, coming home from work the bastard came by the house, and was starting to give me the same line of shit. I went across the street, stepped on his toes, stood about two inches from his face, and told him, I was going to beat the living crap out of him every time I saw him near my house. I left some of my saliva on his face after it was over. Seeing this, one of the neighbors came by, and took him away, saying I wasn't worth it. They should have figured this out from the beginning. After that incident, the insults and stalking came under control. The problem with this approach is, my actions were becoming as reckless as my attacker's. The whole thing could have escalated into something far more serious. Sometimes in a fight, I don't know when to stop. Fortunately, he got the message, before it came to that point.

If I thought I had it bad in our justice system, there were two others, who had it worse. I met them in the waiting room of the prosecutor's office. As in my case, they had just found out the verdict of their recent criminal trial. The plaintiff was a twelve year old rape victim and her mother. The child was raped by a twenty year old neighborhood man. The mother and daughter were clad in rather worn clothes, which made it evident, they were from poor circumstances. The child was crying, and her mother was trying to comfort her. As with my case, the court found her abuser, not guilty. I could take care of myself with the bum, who went after me, but a child. As a parent of low financial means, they can't afford to move out of the neighborhood, so the little girl would be forced to see her attacker every day, with the realization the rape could occur again. How does a mother explain to her daughter, she has no protection under the law? The great United States of America, and they can't protect a skinny 12 year old little girl. I can't help, but wonder, if the parent of the child had money, would the court's verdict be any different?

In fairness to the court, I don't know all the facts behind the case. Maybe there were justifications for the decision that I'm not aware of; maybe the arresting officer didn't have all his ducks in a row; didn't read the alleged attacker his rights or some such little niceties given to suspects by the courts. Also, there is the problem with the rape kit. The kit has all the devices and the procedures to follow, which will prove or disprove the innocence of the accused. It deals with DNA, blood type, etc., which can be taken from the victim's body and clothes for study in a lab to see if there is a match with the alleged attacker. Many rape victims don't report the assault right away, being ashamed of what took place. Washing the clothes they had on during the rape and washing their bodies will obliterate the fluid evidence.

There is a good chance that this is what happened with the little rape victim. Her attacker may have used this as a defense i.e. my word against yours. In any event the victim is now placed in a dangerous position, where this bum can attack her again, and possibly beat her to death the next time. What does her mother do to protect her little girl: buy a gun? Then there is a chance of another felony being committed, murder.

You can see how all this builds and grows, if not dealt with properly from the outset. How does a judge deal with it properly? She uses justice with the law; not only the law alone.

To end our review of the American Justice System at this point would leave out two important components critical in its' successful operation. To summarize, I've written about the plaintiff, the defendant, the suspect, the judge and the police, showing how all of these players interact in the legal system. Little is said about the visitors, who are invited to participate in this playing arena of the court procedure. They aren't the everyday people who work the system, but in my opinion are the most important elements, which make the whole process work. Take them out of it, and the judicial part of democracy won't work. Yet, these volunteers are treated badly. They are harassed, threatened, bullied, inconvenienced and disrespected.

Now if you guessed I'm talking about the witnesses and the jurors as the visitors, you guessed correctly. I've already gone on about witness abuse from the standpoint of a victim, who is also testifying in his own behalf. The non-victim witness is generally treated with the same disrespect, therefore, not wanting to review what has been discussed, I'll limit myself to juror ill-use in this segment and promise you a tale concerning it. This should arouse your interest, and hopefully your indignation. I must warn you ahead of time that my story is rather bizarre and hard to believe, but true in every word, taking place in one day's time. As strange as it may seem, I believe this sort of conduct is happening more than the courts want to admit, and is driving good people away from their jury duty responsibility. The tale, as it goes along, is rather laughable at times, but keep in mind the problem behind it is quite serious, and hence a worthwhile topic to enlighten the reader.

It started raining, as I was driving up to the Municipal Court Building to attend jury duty. My briefcase was sitting on the shotgun seat of the car. Maybe they'll let me do some work, while waiting for a case, I thought to myself. Upon parking my car in the inside parking lot, I started to look for a hat to wear to keep my head dry on my short trip to the main building. All that was available was an old Philadelphia Eagles (pro football team) baseball cap with the old logo on it. It was beat up looking, but good enough to keep my head dry. I put it on, grabbed the briefcase, and hurried along to give myself extra time to find where to go. It had been a while, since my last visit for jury duty, and I had forgotten the layout of the place.

Upon entering the main door, there were several changes made to the lobby area. It was cut off at the end by a counter, which went across the width of the lobby, blocking the entrance to the elevators and the rest of the building. The last time I was there, anyone could walk in like any other office building, and go to wherever you had business. The whole atmosphere had changed; behind the counter were several armed guards and two county policemen. One of them wanted to search through my briefcase.

"Is this necessary," was my reply.

His answer and attitude were direct and rude. "Look bub, I don't make the rules here. You don't let me examine what's in the case, you don't get by the desk. You clear on this?"

"Yes I'm clear on this, but if I have to return it to my car, it will make me late for my appointment." This was another rude answer from the policeman. I was starting to feel the short hairs on the back of my neck rise. Grabbing the case, I left and returned it to my car. It was raining heavier now. Surely my clothes would be wet for several hours as a result. The place is uncomfortable enough without sitting around in damp clothes.

When I returned, a line had formed of people waiting to enter the building. I noticed the lawyers and their clients had no problem getting by the front desk. You could spot the attorneys right away; they had the designer suits on with the expensive Italian made shoes and French cuffed shirts. Their clients looked uncomfortable wearing suits, and had their recent haircuts. The guards and police were polite to this group, calling them 'mister' or 'sir'. The lawyers' brief cases weren't inspected at all, even though some of them did offer to open them for inspection. The other visitors, dressed more informally, were treated in a different manner. Many of them had their summons for jury duty with them, so it was apparent, their purpose there. The guards were openly rude and insulting to them and hurried them along, as if they were cattle. If the guards were insulting, the county policemen were worse.

The one, who previously dealt with me, was not only impolite, but his behavior bordered on being childish and silly, making snide remarks to a few of the older visitors. He was anything but professional. I told him this, when getting by the desk. I didn't use profanity or threats, and simply insisted on better treatment, which I thought was my right as a taxpayer and duty bound citizen. They didn't look at it that way. Six of them jumped me. They put handcuffs on me which were so tight, they took the skin off my wrists, and cut the circulation to my hands. The two Wyatt Earp county cops dragged me off to an interrogation room in another building. More rain on me.

While going along, I asked them if all this was necessary. The one cop answered, "It was. You don't talk to police that way." Notice his answer: he didn't say I was a possible security threat to the courthouse and the occupants. It sounded as if he was getting even with me for saying something to him which he didn't like. He took it personally, which isn't his job. His duty is to protect the building; not get into a fight with one of the jurors. My reply was, "We'll see about that." He yanked the handcuffs, and twisted them a certain way in response to my answer. I could feel the blood from the cuffs' cuts trickle down into the palm of my right hand; the left wrist wasn't cut as badly. I showed no pain, and stopped, making them pause as well. I stared at the one cop indignantly, and I could see it startled him and made him feel uneasy. It was only for a second or two, but I was sure it had an effect. It was I who continued on, pulling the two of them for several steps, until they could regain their bearing. When we got to the interrogation room, they tore through my pockets, and emptied them on the table. The envelope with the summons in it was the last thing they removed. They looked quite upset, when they read it. One of them left immediately, and brought back a plain clothes detective. He told them to take the handcuffs off me, and politely introduced himself, holding out his hand for me to shake. I didn't accept the courtesy. While this was all going on, one of the uniformed cops was quietly writing out a citation for disturbing the peace, before the head cop could say anything to him. He placed it on the table next to me, so I could read it.

I expected the citation; that didn't make me angry. What did upset me was my righteous indignation, which no one seems to possess today. If they did, the others back at the courtroom lobby would be with me, objecting to these punk cops, the way I was. I lit into the detective, the way I promised; careful to maintain enough restraint to state my case clearly, and not sound out of control. However, there was no fear in me for my anger dominated, and took the argument to him. The uniformed policemen didn't say a word. I went on, reminding them of my civil liberties and my right to dissent; that I was a visitor there to perform my civic duty, vital to the legal system, which they were sworn to uphold. In an attempt to quiet me down and gain control of the argument, the plainclothesman told me the whole event was down on video tape.

"That's great," was my reply. "Now there is admissible proof which I can use in civil court, showing I'm telling the truth, if I decide to sue the county."

The mood was beginning to change at that

point.   Politely the plainclothesman responded.
"Now look Mr. Underwood, there is no need to talk
that way.   It appears there was simply a
misunderstanding with my men here, and we are
indeed sorry for any inconvenience it may have
caused you.   There doesn't seem to be any
damage, which I can see."

I interrupted.   Turning to the uniformed
officers, I challenged them.   "Did I at any time
threaten you or anyone or anything connected with
the justice system or the legal procedures currently
in progress at the courthouse?   Remember, before
answering, what happened was recorded on video
tape, which is admissible in a court of law."

There was no answer from them, which
made me think our conversation was now being
recorded.

Turning back to the plainclothesman, "No
damage done, what is this?"   I said, showing him
the cut wrists, and the blood still caked on the
palm of my one hand.

The detective was getting more respectful,
as we went along.   It's funny how the threat of a
law suit will do that to you, especially when you
have a good case.

"Oh, Mr. Underwood let me call the infirmary, and get a nurse up here to dress that for you."

"Not a bad idea; we can use her as a witness."

The nurse was an older woman with a friendly manner, which was welcome after dealing with the policemen. She gently cleaned up the wounds with a peroxide soaked gauze. She asked me if I wanted the wounds dressed. I declined. I told her that I may want her to testify about my injuries in a civil court. She looked over at the detective for approval. He nodded, and told her to give me her name address and phone number. I thanked her, and she left.

"Now look, Mr. Underwood, I want to send you back to the courthouse, but I can't in your present state of mind. What can I do to rectify what happened, and get this straightened out to your satisfaction?"

"Well for starters, you can tear up this citation."

"I'm sorry, Mr. Underwood. I can't do that. Each ticket is pre-numbered, and must be accounted for in that order."

"Well you asked," were my last comments to him.

It was the more under control uniformed cop (the other one was a complete ass), who escorted me back to the main building. He didn't say much to me, but was more polite than when we made the initial trip over. For some unknown reason, I felt sorry for him. I wanted to tell him what his responsibility was towards the public, and how important it is in a democracy; that he, as a law enforcement officer understand the law, and act professionally at all times while administering his duty. I decided my words would only be a waste of my time and energy in delivering them. I said nothing, and sadly walked away, when we reached the courthouse door.

Now after being arrested, you would think the jury attendants wouldn't want to have anything to do with me. Not so. In fact they wanted me for two upcoming cases. But I'm getting ahead of myself. Let me back up a bit; there's more to the story.

It was about 10:30 AM, when the bailiffs gave us our first break, so you can see there was little time elapsed during my interrogation period. I was returned in plenty of time for my first case. The rest rooms were on the first floor only a short distance from the lobby security desk. Out of curiosity, I wanted to see if the cops, who arrested me were still on duty. They weren't; only the building guards were present. It would remain that way for the rest of the day.

When entering the men's room, the area with the washbasins had several people in suits around them washing their hands, and bull – shitting one another. I suppose lawyers need to take a leak the same as anyone else. I made my way back to one of the stalls to take my morning constitutional. Just as I was about to close the stall door, a big colored guy entered the area, where the suits were. He didn't say anything right away. In the meantime, I latched the door and dropped my slacks to do my business. Along about a minute and a half later, he began to mouth off.

"I'm gonna start killing people. Those motherfuckers are no damn good. They ought to die, and I'm gonna kill all of dem."

With that I could hear all of the suits scrambling to get out of the men's room. I was alone now; just me and this crazy guy, who somehow got by the security guards. The same people who previously helped in arresting a poor slob like me, who was invited there to do his civic duty, and meant no harm to anyone. I began to pray.

"Dear Jesus, please get me out of here in one piece, please Lord, please."

I looked through the slit between the door and its' frame. He was visible from there, but I couldn't see if he was armed or not. He continued to ramble on more loudly than before. Couldn't the guards hear him? The men's room wasn't that far from the main desk. Didn't any of the suits notify the guards of this man's behavior and where he was? Apparently not!

He continued on with his tirade. "I'm gonna blow this fuckin place up, and kill all those mother fucking lawyers and judges. They are no fuckin good, and god dam well should die for all the shit dey do to poor people."

(Authors' note: My partner and I want to positively state at this point in the story, our sympathy is more in line with this black man. Not so much with his threats, but with the fact that he was reduced to making them. All brought on by a changed legal system, which has lost touch with justice and fair play. Justice, like the truth, has a way of coming forth, and showing itself; demanding it be heard; apparently it was doing so, as is evidenced by the needed tight security. The courthouse is beginning to look like a tactical zone in a war. By the way, don't blame this on the type of people, who were responsible for 9/11. This story took place prior to that date. Our feeling on the matter is the threat of violence in the courtrooms is American generated.)

I don't know how long this man's harangue lasted. It seemed like an eternity, but it couldn't have been for more than five or ten minutes. Needless to say, when he finally did leave, I thanked Jesus, and got out of there as quickly as my legs could carry me. I immediately went down to the guard's desk to report the incident, and realized why the suits hadn't said anything to the guards: no one was there. Anyone could have walked into the place, planted a bomb, left, and detonated it from across the street with a remote device.

After all I had been through, I was

determined to find out why the station was deserted.   I waited for about ten minutes, before anyone returned to man the security desk; timed it on the wall clock.   He was one of the guards, who with the two bully boy cops, mugged me earlier that morning.   He didn't seem to recognize me, and wasn't even curious why a stranger was standing next to the security desk.   I told him what just happened in the men's room.   His reply was rather odd, or should I say stupid.

"Was he the same guy, who was up on the third floor?   There was a guy up there doing the same thing."   I explained that I wasn't going around the building checking this out.   My business there was that of a juror, who needed to relieve himself.   He only looked at me with a blank stare, and said something under his breath, which I concluded was more to himself than to me.

Confident, I did all I could do about the disturbed black man, I returned to the juror's room. To my amazement I found out that my name was called out to appear on an upcoming case. Taking off my Eagle's cap, I scratched my head trying to make some sense out of all this going on with these jury people.   Less than an hour ago, the police arrested me for (so called) breaking the law, and now, the bailiff had just called out my name to participate in judging a law case. There's something wrong with this picture, I thought to myself. What is with these jury people; do they think I'm going to sit on a jury, and be fair and open minded about a court case after being worked over by two punk cops? It's as if the jury attendants and the police don't communicate with one another. Maybe they don't, or maybe they do and don't care. Shouldn't I be considered an undesirable? Or maybe they don't look at it this way, knowing how the police do this to jurors all the time, I concluded. Here I am ready to judge someone on being guilty or not guilty for a crime, or winning a law suit or not winning one and having done my misdeed only a couple of hours ago. About communication between the police and jury officials, if I were that detective, I wouldn't say anything about the police brutality either. One thing was for certain, everybody in the court room, especially the judges, was going to find out about it from me.

All of the above questions were soon to be answered, but not to my satisfaction. There is a

point before jury selection, where prospective jurors
are allowed to speak with the judge of the
upcoming case, if they feel they are unable to
perform their duty. This is where I decided to
present my case about the police brutality. Both
judges, when I told them my story of how my civil
liberties were abused by the police, appeared
unabashed by it. They excused me immediately,
and refused to listen to the details of my assault,
even to the point of being rude, when I persisted.
What was particularly disturbing, was how ordinary
they treated the complaint, as if it probably
occurred frequently, and they didn't care how a
juror was treated. I couldn't help but wonder, if
the police treated an arrested suspect in this
manner, wouldn't this hurt the case against him?
The judge would listen to the accused's story,
wouldn't he? He would not listen to mine; a
person giving of his time to perform a duty for the
legal system of which the judge was a part. I was
an innocent man, who committed no crime at all,
but to insist on my rights and civil liberties.

    The last words in the Pledge of Allegiance
are, "FOR ALL." These are by far, the saddest
words in the dictum, because they are a terrible lie.

Take the sports figure and movie star O. J. Simpson, for example. Whether guilty or not, he would be on death row now or executed for the crime of murdering his wife and her boyfriend, if he didn't have eleven million dollars to pay out for his court defense. If you are an average American, this ought to alarm you. It did me. In this country a rich person can buy his way out of going to jail, and get away with murder. On the other hand, police can and do trump up charges against a poor person or a person of average means to make their case concerning a crime to get it off the books. It goes both ways. That's what they are paid to do, to solve crimes. Regardless, whether the accused is guilty or not. The proof of this is the few numbers of rich people in jail; statistics on this were recorded earlier. With a good defense attorney, the police wouldn't get away with any quick accumulation of evidence, obtained without a search warrant or the like. Most of it would be challenged and thrown out of court, before the case went to trial. No evidence; no conviction.

Allow me to give you another example of money versus justice. There is a very prominent woman today in a very important position. She has, probably, one of the most respected positions a woman can hold in this country. Apparently, she comes from money. I won't say any more about her background than that, since it says it all. When in her late teen years, she drove her car through a stop sign, ran over, and killed her ex-boyfriend, who recently jilted her. It was ruled by the local police as an accident. In a recent authorized biography about her, the author reveals how this tragic and upsetting accident impacted her life, how hard it was for her to get over it, and put it all behind her. The poor dear did get over it quite well, and is now the toast of the town with people and power at her beck and call. Not only did she get away with the killing, but we're all to feel sorry for her, because she regretted doing it, or so she said. She went through a bad time, as a result of it. How about the victim's family and loved ones; what did they go through? Consider, if she had been just a regular working girl how the crime would be treated. Oh it wasn't a crime, you say; only an auto accident. Look again at the facts in the case. The police in general view a killing as a homicide, if the killer possesses three characteristics: planning, means and motive.

She fit the bill on all three: knew her victim's habits; where he would be at a particular time; the means, an automobile, and the motive, she was jilted. You know the saying, "nothing like a woman scorned"

To broaden your scope concerning the "For All" concept there is no better place to see it in action or lack of action than New York City. The city is made up of five boroughs: Manhattan, Brooklyn, Bronx, Queens, and Staten Island. The overall city is considered a world leader in finance, the arts, and communication. Their port is one of the finest in the world and ranks as the largest port complex on the east coast. New York or the Big Apple, as it is called, is home for the following: United Nations, headquarters for some of the largest corporations in the world, the New York Yankees' baseball team, the Empire State Building, the Statue of Liberty, Broadway stage shows, and many more. New York is also the center of advertising, fashion, publishing, and radio broadcasting in the country. With all its' greatness and power, the city still has similar unemployment, crime and poverty of the average American city. What amazed me, when I first visited Manhattan, was that one could walk from the garment district to Madison Avenue and find himself going from the just getting by type of people to those with immense wealth in a short walk. Money and poverty are coexisting next to each other. It made me so nervous, I just wanted to get out of there as fast as could. You know the old saying: "A nice place to visit, but I wouldn't want to live there." The minute I arrived, I could feel the pull of the town's greatness. It is a city of hopelessness and defeat, and at the same time it possesses an uncanny ability for survival. A foe can kick it in the teeth and knock it down, but in time it will get to its' feet and come back stronger than ever. As I mentioned before, they have the New York Yankees' baseball team; the greatest major league franchise ever assembled, winning more championships than any other team in either league. With all their greatness, many fans still want to see them beaten. To understand the "For All" promise of the Pledge of Allegiance, one can see it more clearly in the Yankees and the city they represent, than anywhere else in the United States. The message conveyed there is clear, "Liberty and Justice for All," is only for those with money. Perhaps that's why most people, other than New Yorkers, want to see the damn Yankees beaten, because they represent the real American theme, "Liberty and Justice for All, Who Are Rich." Maybe by defeating the big money team, the fans receive some satisfaction that the "For All" concept, we desperately want to embrace, is still workable in America. It isn't, but we still don't want to let go of it.

Now after all the negativity we laid on you, the reader, an apology from my partner and I should be in order to balance out our commentary. There must be something nice to say about the good old US of A. Of course there is, but we aren't going to say it, because it will cloud the issues, which must be addressed, and put firmly in your mind. Hopefully, we have done so in this essay; done so, with one exception. What is that exception, you may want to ask, or maybe you don't want to ask; maybe you don't care. If you don't, then this is the most sorrowful of everything said, for not caring hurts this country more than any evil. In fact, indifference is the ultimate wrong in a Republic, and the crux of what we are trying to enumerate in The Pledge. By some miracle we still have a republic, which exists in spite of the apathy concerning our responsibilities towards it. Thank God for this, when you say your evening prayers. Yes, you are still allowed to pray. However, your republic can slip right through your fingers, if you don't work to keep it. Go out and vote; fifty percent turnout is pathetic. Remember, it counts more than you think. Write your congressman, when you're upset about something going on in the government. Make your representative work. Maybe we'll get something worthwhile out of this body, if enough pressure is put on them. Mumbling under your breath about a problem, doesn't count for anything other than high blood pressure.

To make it clear about the one exception, we spoke of in the last paragraph: it is living up to the commitment of our founding fathers, who drafted the US Constitution. This document isn't just a group of written laws. It is much more. It is a responsibility placed on you, the citizen, to take part in the running of this republic of ours. Yes, fellow Americans it belongs to us. In return for our participation, the drafters promised a system of laws, which protects our rights of life, liberty and the pursuit of happiness for all.

Our warning is that this promise is slowly eroding away, and in fact slipping through our fingers. It happens slowly, like a cancer growth, and one day it will be gone. For me it was worth all the pain, bruises, and humiliation I received in testing out the American system of Justice to bring it to your attention. Please take all of this to heart, and be aware, if they can do this to me, they can do it to you, too. Even though I didn't like what I experienced and saw, I concluded it is better to know, than not to know.

End of: THE PLEDGE

VICTIMS RIGHTS

"The whole crowd cried out, '"Kill him (referring to Jesus Christ)!   Set Barabbas (a murderer and thief) free for us!"'"

Luke 23:18

The saddest essay my partner and I had to write is by far this one, since it exposes the American Judicial System for its' deliberate refusal to administer the laws of this nation.   This is a responsibility they were sworn to uphold.   I've documented much of their failure in the last chapter from my own personal experience in the system as a victim, so there shouldn't be any need to rehash this treatment, but I'll refer to it now and then. What we want to do in this paper is to understand why victim's rights have diminished in recent years; studying it from where it all began to the present day.   We will attempt to understand, why the Supreme Court would go against established Common Law edicts such as: "ignorance of the law is no excuse," and "notifying the police before leaving the scene of a crime."   Both are imperative in ascertaining guilt in a criminal case.

For some unknown reason these are now overlooked in a court of law. In my case the defendant did leave the crime scene without calling the police, which, as it turned out, had no bearing on the final verdict, but should have. Also, isn't "reading an arrested suspect his rights," the complete opposite of, "ignorance of the law is no excuse?" It sounds as if the courts are making up the law, as they go along. If this is true then this country is in deep trouble. In addition to this, is the question of checks and balances between the three branches of government i.e. the legislative, judicial, and the executive. What are the other two branches doing to bring the court in line with the general good and will of the people, provided for them in the Constitution of this nation? Or, are Congress and the Chief Executive part of the problem? This is especially worrisome, since these two branches are directly linked to the public. If the people can't go to them, then what can they do? I should also add that appointment to the Supreme Court is a lifetime position, and can only be ended by the appointee's resignation or death. There is no accountability for these members regarding their decisions. They can be made with or without the will of the people, and become law from the date enacted.

A good way of understanding a problem is to study the history of it, and most times, along the way the "why" will surface. Perhaps what can be done to turn a problem around will also surface. In order for us all to be on the same page concerning what the problem is, it has been established in the previous chapter on justice that there is a lack of victim's rights in the American Court System.

(2)Miranda vs. Arizona, 1966 was a landmark decision by the Earl Warren, Supreme Court (5 to 4), overturning the conviction ruling on the case against Ernesto Miranda, who confessed to a crime during police questioning without knowing he had the right to have an attorney present. The Court ruled that criminal suspects must be warned of their rights, before they are questioned by police. These rights (under the 14th amendment) are: the right to remain silent, to have an attorney present, and if the suspect cannot afford an attorney, one will be appointed by the state. The police must also warn suspects that what they say can be used against them in a court of law. Miranda was retried without the confession and convicted. (2)Source: TIME Almanac 2003

Although he was still found guilty of the same crime in a retrial, Miranda's impact on the Justice system in America remained. A cheap crook and thug literally turned American justice around, giving the criminal suspect a serious advantage over his victim in a court of law. My experience relates this in detail. It does the following: one, evidence (proof of guilt) isn't admissible in court if it is obtained without following a certain procedure. The judge didn't allow the doctor's written testimony, who checked me over at the hospital, since he wasn't subpoenaed by the prosecution. Two, a victim isn't considered a victim, only a witness, and not a reliable one by court standards. Three, the criminal (out on bail) can harass and threaten the victim, and the latter will not receive police protection, because it could jeopardize the case against him. Four, the victim isn't advised of his rights. Five; the victim has no voice in determining if the case will be judged by his peers (a jury) or by the bench. Six, (in my situation) I wasn't advised, who would be testifying against me in the case. There were four witnesses, who were total strangers, who testified against me.

I assumed they were friends of the accused, and were there simply to manifest their belief in his character, since they did not witness the attack. This evidently was accepted by the court, because the prosecutor asked me if I wanted to get up on the stand and defend myself against their accusations. What happened here: I was placed on trial. I had already made my statement against the suspect. Legally this was my only responsibility. Why weren't my friends allowed to get up on the witness stand, and testify in my behalf? Justice would dictate that I should likewise have the same privileges as my attacker.

It is clear from the above, the alleged criminals have all the advantages in the American court system, and that brings me back to, "why." Why would a cheap criminal, like Miranda be given all this consideration, leading up to a Supreme Court decision? Was Earl Warren just stupid in making it, or did he have a reason? Why would the man deliberately change criminal law, giving the advantage to the criminals, and thereby victimizing the victims and the American public in general? Why would the other branches of the government allow it? I realize these questions were posed previously, but some questions are important enough to ask about a second time.

My partner and I came to a conclusion about, "why," by asking another question: "what if Warren's decision wasn't justice motivated?" If our conclusions were correct about the United States being The Money Country, then wouldn't it hold that the U. S. Supreme Court would likewise be money motivated?

(5)What do we know about Earl Warren? 1891 – 1974. He was Chief Justice of the US Supreme Court from 1953 to 1969, graduated from University of California 1912; was Attorney General of California 1939 to 1943 and Governor 1943 to 1953 and unsuccessful Republican Party Vice Presidential candidate 1948. He was well known for three events in his career as a Justice on the Supreme Court, which impacted American living: one, Brown v. Board of Education (1954), in which public school segregation was ruled unconstitutional; two, (1963/1964) headed the official inquiry into the assassination of US President John F. Kennedy, which concluded there was no evidence of a conspiracy and Lee Harvey

Oswald acted alone in killing President Kennedy. It also found that Jack Ruby the Dallas restaurant owner, who shot and killed Oswald, also acted alone, and three, Miranda v. Arizona, which helped define the 14th Amendment of the US Constitution (or so was his conclusion; four other members on the court didn't agree).   While we're on the subject of 'not agreeing with him', his report and findings on the Kennedy assassination also came under close examination and widespread criticism. In 1979 a congressional committee concluded, on the basis of acoustical evidence, that two gunman had fired at Kennedy.

(5)Source: The Concise Columbia Encyclopedia, Second Edition.

Not a very impressive resume, if you ask me.   He did two terrible disservices to our country: one, in the Kennedy murder conspiracy decision, he destroyed the trust between the government and the people it represented, and two, in the Miranda decision, he set the precedent, which would allow known criminals to walk the streets, taking away good American's civil liberties.   In short he turned American living into a living hell.

Now through history, we found out who Earl

Warren was, and what he did to victim's rights. With a little more study of history, we will discover why he did it, and perhaps discover what could be done to undo the damage caused by his court. Beginning with the Miranda decision of 1966 to the present, the Supreme Court has been dominated by Republican Party Justices. From 1968 when Richard M. Nixon was elected President of the United States to the present, the Oval Office has been mostly occupied by Republican Party nominees. My count is seven terms GOP vs. three terms for the Democrats. During this time the Democrats appointed only three Justices. This gives the Republicans a very clear majority on the Court. The mandate from the founding fathers of this country is, the Supreme Court of the United States will be above politics, and show no favoritism to either side. Has the Court in this period of time acquiesced to this mandate? I don't believe so. The most brazen example of their refusal to do so, was the Al Gore vs. G. Walker Bush election, where the Court reversed a decision by the Florida Supreme Court to allow manual recounts of ballots in some of their counties. As a result of the Court's decision,

Bush won the presidency. It was the first time in the country's history that the US Supreme court determined the outcome of a presidential election – (5 to 4). This is too much power given to one branch of the government, and clearly a conflict of interest, since it goes against separation of powers. Why the Democratic Party didn't challenge this, is beyond my understanding. Not only was it in their better interest to do so, it was their duty according to the law. If the Supreme Court isn't controlled and made accountable for their decisions, their power becomes omnipotent.

Getting back to the Republican Party. The GOP is the party of big business and the money interests in this country. I'm not implying that there is anything wrong with this; there isn't, provided the checks and balances of our leadership are applied for the better interest of the American people. Without the Republican Party, our nation wouldn't have a two party system, and would come under dictatorial rule. However, stepping outside of the two party system and taking a close look at the Supreme Court wielding their power, as they have since the 1960's, they are starting to look dictatorial. This is what concerns my partner and me.

Let's take our postulation further, and look at the victims' rights issue from the political point of view (and money, of course), and not try to make sense out of it from the justice side. When we did, it began to make sense. Here are some of the ugly probabilities that we came up with in our hypothesis.

If an accused criminal has money, it is assumed he is a tax payer. Putting that person in jail, keeps him from paying taxes, and then every time he defends himself in court, he pays lawyer's fees, which keeps them rich. Incarcerating that person means no tax revenues from him and the cost of him being locked up, which is about eighty thousand dollars a year, paid out by the state. If the accused is poor, it is assumed he pays little or no taxes at all, and instead is on welfare, which is a financial burden to the state. Also, this person most likely will have children, and they will become a burden to the state, and add to the community's undesirables. It pays the government to incarcerate such an individual, and get him out of the way. One other reason, the poor person is most likely to rob convenience stores in or near his community, which are run by big businesses.

This leads us to the victim. The only way to keep the accused from going to jail is to victimize the victim. Discredit him/her, and turn the trial into accusing the victim. A defense attorney can always find some scum to get up and lie on the witness stand for the fee accorded him for his time, and this is legal. The court will believe him, but won't allow the victim the same right.

So you see Earl Warren wasn't as stupid, as history makes him look. We can call him a lot of things, but stupid isn't one of them. We believe he was part of a plan, which was orchestrated by the Republican Party to gain control of the power base in the United States, which is in place at this time. It started with the assassination of President John Kennedy and his brother Robert then went downhill from there. What was the reason for the two assassinations? They were afraid of the Kennedy's, and knew either one as President would sanction the Supreme Court for their questionable decisions. The Kennedy's had the courage to do so, and had the support of the American people. Oh, by the way, look at the dates of the assassinations: President Kennedy (Democrat) was assassinated November 1963; his brother was killed in Los Angeles June 1968, while running for the Democratic Presidential nomination. More history: in March, 1968 President Johnson (Democrat) surprised the country with his announcement, he would not seek reelection. January 1969 President elect Richard M. Nixon (Republican) was inaugurated as the 37th President of the United States and was sworn in by Earl Warren, Chief Justice of the US Supreme Court (Republican). September, 1974 President Gerald Ford (Republican) grants an unconditional pardon to Nixon for any crimes he might have committed during his presidency. Talk about name dropping. Are we to believe all of this was just a coincidence? It sounds to us that this period in Presidential history has defined the fall of human rights in America. It was calculated and acted upon with the approval of prominent figures in each party.

One more thing, why was Earl Warren appointed to the court in the first place? What background did he have as a judge? None. He was a politician (ran unsuccessfully on the

Republican ticket for Vice President of the United States 1948 and was Governor of California 1943 to 1953). The Court members should be above and separate from politics; evidently Warren wasn't.

What can be done with the Supreme Court to get it back where it should be in relation to the other branches of power? Plenty. First off, Congress should introduce a bill stating that appointees of the Court must be free of political affiliations, and have no ambitions about running for a major elected office of the government. Secondly, a court member's tenure should not be a lifetime job. There isn't a position in America, which I know of, which is for a lifetime. Why should a judge of the American people have this privilege? If a limit can be placed on how long the President of the United States can serve (ten years maximum), why can't a limit be placed on Justices?

Now what can be done to correct the damages caused by the US Supreme Court against victims? Simple. Getting back to the US Congress, this body must address the problem, and act on it by passing a bill, which brings victim's rights in balance with those of the accused.   The Congress doing nothing is abetting the problem.   Are they?

End of: VICTIMS RIGHTS

THE COMPARISON

There is an old saying, "History has a way of repeating itself." Like all old sayings, they hang around and become old, because there is so much truth in them. There are two pieces of history, I'd like to share with you, which bear repeating; the one mirrors the other. The two greatest empires of all time are: the Roman Empire, which conquered all the known world, approximately two thousand years ago, and secondly, the American Empire, which today influences the entire world. "The two empires have much in common," my college professor once told me, when I questioned the man on the subject. He went on to answer my question in more detail, describing the two empires' military conquests, the layout of their government and the two party system, their innovations, and many more similarities. Several years would pass, before I realized, there was one more likeness, which he failed to mention. The time of our discussion was shortly after President Kennedy's assassination. It was easy for the both of us to miss this, since history hadn't developed on the subject. History has a way of exposing the truth, which I postulated on in the previous chapter, and will refer to in upcoming chapters. It will be used to shed light on The Comparison which my college professor and I missed, back in the sixties.

Rome had (Caius) Julius Caesar, 102 to 44 BC; America had John Fitzgerald Kennedy, 1917 to 1963 AD. I would like to begin with a short history of Julius Caesar, and then follow doing the same with John Kennedy. The comparison between the two is astounding. We will then end with what was missed.

(5)Julius Caesar (statesman and general) was born into one of the oldest patrician or wealthy families, the Julian gens. Contrary to his birthrights, he affiliated himself with the democratic or popular party. He began his political career as a member of this party and remained faithful to it. In 69 BC he helped General Pompey establish the supreme command for the war in the east. He returned to Rome from Spain is 68 BC, and continued to back the enactment of popular legislation, and to prosecute senatorial extortionists. In 63 BC, with the help of Sosigenes, he undertook the reform of the calendar. The result was one of the greatest contributions to history, the Julian calendar.

In 60 BC, Caesar organized the first
Triumvirate, a coalition made up of Pompey,
commander of the Army; Marcus Licinius Crassus,
the wealthiest man in the empire, and himself.
With this backing he firmly established (in 58 to 49
BC) his reputation in the Gallic Wars. As part of
this, he made explorations into Britain in 55 and 54
BC, and defeated the Britons. When these
campaigns ended, Caesar brought all of Gaul
under Roman control, which established him as
one of the great military commanders of all time.
As with all great leaders Caesar made enemies;
one of them was Pompey. On 49 BC, Caesar and
his armies crossed the Rubicon and entered Italy,
where civil war broke out. Fighting his way
through it, he pressed on triumphantly to Rome.
At Pharsala (48 BC) he defeated Pompey, forcing
him to flee to Egypt, where he was killed. Caesar
having pursued him there, decided to remain, living
with Cleopatra, establishing her firmly on the
Egyptian throne.

On his return to Rome, he set about
reforming the average person's living conditions,
through Agrarian legislation, and improving housing

accommodations. He became dictator for life in 44 BC. His popularity with the people, and dictatorial powers raised much concern and resentment. Ironically, it wasn't his enemies involved in the conspiracy against him, which led to his assassination. It was his friends and protégés, among them Cimber, Casca, Cassius and Brutus, who together stabbed Caesar to death on the Senate house floor in 44 BC (Ides of March).

The man was indeed gifted, regardless of whatever his critics said about him. His commentaries on the Gallic Wars (seven books), and on the Civil War (three books) are literary masterpieces. He was much the ladies' man; besides Cleopatra, he was married three times to Cornelia, Paopeia, and Calpurnia.

(11)John Fitzgerald Kennedy (1917 to 1963) was the 35th president of the United States (1961 to 1963). He was the second oldest son in the prestigious and famous Kennedy family from Massachusetts. Jack (his nickname) served with distinction as commander of a PT boat in the Pacific portion of the Second World War. After the war he was elected to a seat in the US Congress representing the state of Massachusetts (1947 to

1953); running on the Democratic ticket.   In 1952 he won a seat in the US Senate. A year later he married Jacqueline Lee Bouvier. He won his party's presidential nomination in 1960, and went on to defeat Republican Richard M. Nixon, becoming the nation's youngest president at the age of 43 years old. The New Frontier was the name of his domestic program; it called for tax reform, federal aid to education, medical care for the aged, and the extension of civil rights. However, most of his reforms were held up in Congress, and Cold War crises abroad occupied much of his time. Although criticized by some for aborting the Cuban Bay of Pigs invasion in 1961, he remained popular with the American people, receiving a high approval rating from them. His administration was dubbed, "the return to Camelot", liking it to the Arthurian legend, the seat of King Arthur's court.

In the fall of 1962 American reconnaissance planes photographed Soviet missile bases in Cuba, which developed into the Cuban Missile Crises. President Kennedy ordered a naval blockade of the island, and demanded the immediate removal of the missiles. The USSR would eventually capitulate. The event would establish the young president as a no nonsense leader, facing the seasoned veteran leader Nikita Khrushchev, and winning out against him, without bloodshed.

On the minus side of the Kennedy administration, he would involve the US in the Viet Nam Civil War, sending 16,000 advisors there on the side of the south. Realizing the folly of this involvement, he promised many of his closest advisors, he would remove them, when reelected.

Another minus, Jack Kennedy, although apparently happily married to Jacqueline, did have an appetite for other women. It was rumored he had an affair with Marylyn Monroe, as well as others.

Getting back to the plus side: Kennedy established the Alliance for Progress to give aid to Latin America, and created the Peace Corps. He also pressed hard to achieve racial integration in the South.

On November 22, 1963, President Kennedy was shot and killed in Dallas, Texas. Vice President Lyndon Johnson followed him as president of the country. His first official act was to create the Warren Commission, headed by Chief Justice Warren of the Supreme Court, to investigate the assassination. The commission concluded it was the work of a single gunman. This however was refuted in 1979 by the House Select Committee on Assassinations, relying in part on acoustical evidence, which proved that two gunmen fired on the President. Their conclusion was that a conspiracy did take place that day, and it may have involved organized crime.

(11)Note: Kennedy was much the intellectual, and had concern for culture and learning. He attracted a number of intellectuals to Washington during his presidency, and authored two books of his own; one of which (Profiles in Courage) won a Pulitzer Prize.

Source: (5) The Concise Columbia Encyclopedia, Second Edition

(11)The American Nation – A History of the United States

This is what my college professor and I missed. All of the above data should end The Comparison between the two great leaders, if you are looking at it from the surface, and not from cause and effect. However for us, we believe in going further, since there is one more important comparison left unanswered: was Kennedy, like his counterpart, murdered by colleagues? To properly give the American people closure concerning his death, and we consider it in this realm, since he was loved; this question must be addressed. As an aid to our attempt, we through history and logic, will structure the Kennedy assassination(s), and who had the most to gain by the killing(s). The extra length of the reading is additionally worthwhile, because it establishes a key turning point in the direction the powerbase of our government would take from that point to the present. We stand by the exhaustive research we've done on the assassination, which supports our conclusion, that Kennedy, like Caesar was killed by colleagues. I realize this goes against the Warren Commission Report and later the House Select Committee on Assassinations conclusions. The former is now believed to be a complete farce; the latter shows some truth in bringing to light, there was more than one shooter in the killing. Blaming organized crime for the conspiracy is as ludicrous as the Warren Report in its' entirety.

Using common sense to justify our conclusions, we asked: "What in the world would the mob gain by killing Jack Kennedy and then a few years later killing his brother? Nothing! The last thing this element wanted to do was to bring attention to themselves. They knew they could continue in business on the local level, by bribing police and judges, as they always had done. Why go to the trouble of killing the President of the United States and his Attorney General, drawing attention of the American public to their illegal activities? It doesn't make any sense.

What does make sense is, when you ask the question, "who had the most to gain by the Kennedy deaths?" By the way, we believe the two murders are connected, and will proceed with this assumption, using history to verify our conclusions. Who actually did the shootings is irrelevant; these scumbags are everywhere. In a murder conspiracy, where the investigation will be controlled, all of this can be arranged, as well as the cover up. When we studied the assassinations and the political events surrounding them, we came up with four men, who had a lot to benefit by their deaths. Let me make it perfectly clear, we are not accusing them of these murders, since we don't have proof of their guilt. We are simply saying they all had a motive, and the connections for arranging the murders.

(12)First on the list is Lyndon Baines Johnson (1908 to 1978), who became the 36th President of the United States, when President Kennedy was assassinated on November 22, 1963. To jog your memory of the man, Johnson was elected US Senator from Texas 1948, and became the majority leader after the 1954 elections. After losing the 1960 presidential nomination to Jack Kennedy, he agreed to be his running mate. Much to his credit, he, as president, skillfully prodded Congress to pass many of the Kennedy programs, which included a sizeable tax cut, and a sweeping Civil Rights Act, along with a Medicare bill, federal aid to education, and increased anti-poverty programs. On the minus side, he escalated the Viet Nam War from the 16,000 advisors Kennedy authorized to as many as 550,000 American troops in 1969. This resulted in widespread opposition in Congress and the public. When questioned about it, he often blamed his predecessor, calling Viet Nam, "the war he inherited." He seldom, if ever, mentioned the lucrative contracts awarded to the large defense manufacturers, who were the only people in the war coming out ahead.

Being much older than the Kennedy brothers, I believe, and I think Johnson did too, that he wouldn't reach the highest political office in the land, as long as the Kennedy's were alive. Also, being the Vice President, Johnson knew the exact route the Dallas motorcade would take on that fateful day, and conveniently wasn't in the same car as Jack and his wife. He wasn't fired upon in the attack; how fortunate it was for him. Evidently the sole target was the President.

The second person on my list is Allen Welch Dulles (1893 to 1969); brother of President Eisenhower's Secretary of State John Foster Dulles, and first civilian director of the Central Intelligence Agency or CIA (1963 to 1971). He had good reasons for wanting President Kennedy dead: survival of the CIA, which Kennedy threatened to disband, and revenge for being fired by the man. He also had the opportunity and means: the CIA, whose practice back then, was illegal covert actions, which included assassinations.   Limitations have since been placed on the agency, coordinating their domestic counter-intelligence with the Federal Bureau of Investigation, and subject to the Attorney General's approval.

The restrictions were put in place by the 1978 Jimmy Carter Presidential Executive Order. Evidently the agency was beginning to get out of control, as was evidenced by their involvement in the Watergate affair and other unlawful domestic spying.   Additionally the agency was criticized for taking an active role in the internal affairs of foreign governments.

Dulles, although not in charge of the CIA at the time of the Kennedy murder, was certainly knowledgeable of their operations, and could have arranged the assassination through contacts in the agency.   Think about it for a minute: how could some fool like Oswald fire successfully on a moving car, hitting the President squarely in the head from that distance away; using an inferior weapon?   It can't be done.   I know; I'm an ex-Marine; it's our business to know about guns, and marksmanship.

This brings me to the third person on the

list: Earl Warren (1891 to 1974), 14th Chief Justice of the US Supreme Court (1953 to 1969). He was appointed to the court by President Eisenhower, who wanted a conservative justice and commented that, "he (Warren) represents the kind of political, economic, and social thinking that I believe we need on the Supreme Court... He has a national name for integrity, uprightness, and courage that, again, I believe we need on the court." Warren, as it turned out, would be just the opposite of what Ike had in mind; he was quite liberal in some of his decisions on the Court. Consequently Eisenhower later is said to have remarked, Warren's appointment was, "the biggest damned-fool mistake I ever made."

So you can see how easily Warren could adjust to a situation, and change his opinion of it to benefit himself in some manner. When President Johnson came to him to head the commission on the death of Kennedy, the Chief Justice was willing to cooperate. It is the writers' opinion that Warren would turn out to be the main force in the murder cover-up, since legal action couldn't be taken at the point of his involvement. What Warren and President Johnson had in common was, they didn't have a party ideology; you could call their thinking apolitical. They did whatever would give them power. (Note: Allow me to qualify the difference between a political party hat versus a manipulator, and having a party ideology. The former is a selfish blind commitment; the latter is a heartfelt belief). Remember Johnson was an expert arm−twister, when he was the Senate Majority Leader. He had a way of convincing many in the Congress (both parties) to cooperate, and in return would give them something they wanted. He was a negotiator; we used to call them a horse dealer. What was it that Warren wanted in return for his cooperation? He wanted more power. Power to pass laws, which he knew the Kennedys wouldn't allow. Understand one thing, when I say Kennedys; there wasn't just Jack alone; there was Robert and also Ted, who were politically minded. It was feared by their opposition, these three men would follow each other to the Presidency. With the Kennedy's out of the way, and Johnson as President, the Court would be free to enact any laws they wanted. This would make the Supreme Court very powerful. The laws they would pass in the future would literally change the American life style. We believe for the worse.

My partner and I already listed their laws before, but we will briefly go over them again to refresh your memory.

Supreme Court ruled 8 – 1 on June 17, 1963 that laws requiring recitation of the Lord's Prayer or bible verses in public schools were unconstitutional; based on separation of church and state. My partner confided: a lot of great leaders come out of the church i.e. Martin Luther King, Jesse Jackson and others. The way of controlling their influence is to do it at the elementary and high school levels. This was the theory of the communist controlled countries; take away the people's religious freedom. Belief in God unites people, and gives them a purpose to do right. To maintain power, the state must remove the ultimate power from the minds of the populace: God. You all know what happened to communism, and the Roman Empire for that matter. Again history repeating itself.

1966 Miranda vs. Arizona – Defined the due process clause of the 14th amendment, i.e. read the accused his rights, etc. The reasoning behind the law was discussed earlier in Victim's

Rights.

1973 Roe vs. Wade – legalized abortion. It was aimed at population control, especially of poor people.

My partner and I concluded, the power base of the Johnson era was 'back room' politics, which was closed to the public. These men shared the power; they were apolitical, not representing a constituent base. This is the first step in having a one party system; power becoming too powerful for their own good, or for the good of the people. Ironically, or perhaps on purpose the power brokers of the era seemed to be the very people on the Warren Commission:

.. Earl Warren, Chief Justice of the US Supreme Court

.. Richard Russell, Jr. (D – GA), Senator US Congress

.. John Sherman Cooper (R – KY), Senator US Congress

.. Hale Boggs (D – LA), Representative US Congress

.. Gerald Ford (R – MI), Representative US Congress

.. Allen Welsh Dulles, former Director of the

Central Intelligence Agency

.. John J. Mc Cloy, former President of the World Bank.

All of these men on the list were at the dictate of LBJ, who rose to the office of Chief Executive making the power structure complete. You could say they were all team players, and the defiant Kennedy's weren't. Being team players didn't make them qualified to conduct a murder investigation. As far as I know none of them had background in this line of work. Secondly, one must question why Allen Welsh Dulles was on the commission. As I suggested before, he should have been a prime suspect in the Kennedy murder. He had motive, means and opportunity to commit the crime. His background in the assassination business is well documented through the agency (CIA) he headed. He developed some of their practices, which were unscrupulous and illegal. From the outset of the aborted Cuban invasion, Dulles faced increasing criticism from the President, who insisted the director gave him incorrect information concerning the operation, and laid blame on him for its' failure. As a result he and two of his Deputy Directors, Richard M.

Bissell, Jr. and Charles Cabell were forced to resign. Kennedy didn't trust the agency, and made it clear that he intended to dismantle it.

Before moving on to the fourth person on the 'Most to Gain List,' I want to say something about the least known member of the Commission, but the most interesting, John Jay McCloy. Briefly, he was born in Philadelphia, PA (1895 – 1989), educated at Amherst College, and received a law degree from Harvard Law School. He was a prominent attorney and banker, who served as Assistant Secretary of War during World War II, president of the World Bank, and US High Commissioner for Germany. Why was he on the Warren Commission? I guess he represented the money side of the power structure. What interested my partner and I the most was his friendship with Allen Dulles. McCloy at first was suspicious of the lone gunman theory. However on a trip (in the Spring 1964) with Dulles to visit the scene of the Kennedy murder, he changed his thinking on the matter, and was won over to the case against Oswald. It was Mc Cloy, who convinced the others on the commission of this. He concluded, and it was so noted in the report, "any possible evidence of a conspiracy was beyond the reach of all America's investigatory agencies– principally, the Federal Bureau of Investigation and the Central Intelligence Agency – as well as the Commission itself."   Weather the former is true or not, we'll never know.

(12)Source: Wikipedia, the free encyclopedia – Earl Warren, 11/2/2009

(5)And now the fourth person on the list is Richard M. Nixon (1913 – 1994).   To understand why we put the 37th president (1969 –1974) on the Most to Gain List, one must put their deductive reasoning to work.   We will guide you through this, but first it might help to give you some political background on the man.   "Tricky Dick," as his enemies affectionately nicknamed him, was a US Representative (1947 – 1951) from California, where he gained prominence for his investigation of Alger Hiss.   In his brief tenure in the US Senate (1951 – 1953) he attacked the Democratic administration as being pro socialist.   On a party fast track, he was nominated and elected as Vice– President with Dwight D. Eisenhower in 1952 and 1956.   In 1960 he ran for president, and was defeated by John Kennedy in the Presidential race. In 1962 he was defeated in his home state in the California gubernatorial election. At this point he was on a losing streak, and it was feared his political career was all but over. Two events took place, which would keep his sinking career from sinking totally: one, President Johnson decided not to run for a second term, and two, Robert F. Kennedy seeking the Democratic Presidential nomination, was shot and killed after winning the California primary, which would have made him his party's front runner. Those two happenings conveniently eliminated Nixon's competition for the office. Again let me repeat, my partner and I don't believe in coincidences. From that point on, the previous loser became a winner: he won the presidency in 1968, running on the promise to end the Viet Nam War, and again in 1972. He was rather slow in keeping his promise to end the war. Finally in 1973 a cease fire agreement was signed in Paris, France which allowed US troops to withdraw from the beleaguered country. Like his predecessor, he kept the war going, which gives a hint that he believed in the military/industrial complex. You may recall his previous boss,

Dwight D. Eisenhower gave a warning in his farewell speech concerning this liaison. Another incident occurred to illustrate Nixon's character: investigation into the Watergate Affair revealed corruption in his administration. In 1974 the US House of Representatives began impeachment proceedings against the president on the grounds of obstruction of justice, abuse of power, and failure to comply with congressional subpoenas. Pressured by this threat, he became the first US President to resign his office.

(5)Source: The Concise Columbia Encyclopedia – Second Edition

End of: THE COMPARISON

REAGAN

Ronald Wilson Reagan was the fortieth President of the United States; served from 1981 to 1988. He was born in 1911 Tampico, Illinois, which made him the oldest President ever to occupy the oval office. Up until his political ambitions started, which essentially began when he ran for and was elected governor of California (1967 to 1974), he was a motion picture actor. This was another first for the man; no other American president ever reached the office, having an acting resume. He was divorced from his first wife, actress Jane Wyman (1949) and remarried to Nancy Davis (1952), who was also in the acting profession. This was another first for the man. Before his presidency, it was considered a political impossibility to be elected to this office. Reagan was a man, who would attain the office, even though he was a divorced candidate. He overcame many obstacles to reach his goals. One of these obstacles was his humble beginnings in Tampico and Dixon, Illinois, which we will not address here, but only mention it to show the man's resolve.   A person either overcomes his obstacles or he doesn't, and it is enough said that Reagan certainly overcame his.   Ron's older brother Neil (whom he was very close with) and wife Nancy had money, and connections. This is where it all begins with one's trip to the Presidency of the United States.   I'm not condemning this; maybe I should, but unfortunately this is how the system works. It takes money to gain power, since this is the money country.

Up until the point of the man's passing away, I had forgotten about the fortieth President. The many accolades being said about him at his demise, rekindled my interest in the man.   It appears some people become great, when they die, and so it was with Ronald Reagan.   Many prominent people (of both parties, and others outside of politics) were saluting the man, and his excellent accomplishments during his time in office. I couldn't agree with their memory of him.   Maybe they were just saying all this to be nice to the man's family. That's all well and good, but were their assessments meaningful?   This is what my partner and I were concerned with and we were motivated enough to dig up (no pun intended) what information was available on Mr. Reagan to see if all the fanfare about him was deserved.

Up until Reagan raised his right hand and swore to enforce and uphold the laws of the United States of America as President, I had little interest in him, as I intimated earlier.   Although I knew of Reagan as an actor, I considered him as washed up in that profession, which he was.   When he took office, he immediately affected my life and that of my family, both financially and in my career. Every goal and aspiration I ever had would rest on what this man did as President, and every President, who would follow him.   Harry S. Truman, our thirty third President once said, "If you (the American people) don't have the President on your side, then you have no representation in the running of this country."   Did Reagan live up to the Truman legacy?   We will look into that, but I can't promise you a lot, since he did very little constructively.

Following up on different eulogies of some very prominent people, they appear to be very nice, as I said before, but lacking concerning his accomplishments in behalf of the American people. Here is a sampling of their remarks.

Pennsylvania Governor Ed Rendell (Democrat): "His most enduring legacy will be, he lifted the county's spirits and morale at a time, when it was desperately needed. All America should be grateful for his service and commitment."

Sorry Ed, I didn't get the same feeling you did. After eight years of his leadership, I had enough. My spirits weren't lifted at all.

Pennsylvania State Senator Tommy Tomlinson (Republican): "He led our country through a dark period in its history with style, intellect and humor. As a public official, I often reflect on his terms of service for inspiration. He will be greatly missed by freedom loving people everywhere."

Don't agree Tommy; I'm one freedom loving person, who wasn't inspired by him; only hurt.

Outside Pennsylvania, the United Nations' secretary General Kofi Annan said of Reagan, "he will be remembered for his leadership and resolve during a period of momentous change in world affairs, as well as for the warmth, grace and humor with which he conducted affairs of state."

Dear Kofi, Reagan's warmth, grace and

humor with which he conducted affairs of state were provided by his wife Nancy. I'll say this about him, he married well.

This all sounded very proper: "I don't want to speak ill of the dead," way of saying nothing concrete about his Presidency. As I said before, my partner and I wanted to know more about the man than what was politely expressed upon his death. Did he live up to the Truman legacy, and to the challenge he gave to the American people, when debating with President Carter? "Ask yourself, am I any better off after his (pointing to Carter) term in office?" Good question, every voter should ask this, when entering the voting booth to cast their ballot for an incumbent president. Before evaluating this, and giving Reagan a report card about his time in office, we wanted to go back to before he was elected, and review what made him politically what he was. Knowing this will give you the man's motives for his actions in power.

President Reagan was apolitical, just as some of his recent predecessors were i.e. Presidents Johnson and Nixon. In other words, he was affiliated with whatever party would achieve his political goals and aspirations. He had no ideology or belief in a political agenda. You may recall the referral to this in our previous paper written about Chief Justice Earl Warren, who was for any cause that would give him power. The problem with this is, it robs the American people of the two party system, which is vital to the political success of the American electoral process. So with Reagan, he started off as a Democrat: in 1948 he supported Harry Truman for president, in 1952 he campaigned as a Democrat for Eisenhower, and he wound up as a Republican in 1962, campaigning for Barry Goldwater, and Richard Nixon. We understand this is his right to do so, but on the other hand, one must ask, just exactly where do this man's political affiliations stand. What does he believe?

(13)In order to understand the political Ronald Reagan, you should know more about his second wife Nancy, who was responsible in a large part for making her husband apolitical. She was born Anne Francis Robbins on July 6, 1921. Her mother, Edith Luckett was a movie star in the silent film era, and gave her daughter the nickname Nancy. When her parent's divorce was final, her mother married a prominent neurosurgeon, Loyal Davis on 1929, and moved along with her daughter into his home in Chicago. The teenager, Nancy, came to know and love him as her father. She, while still in her teens, tracked down her biological father; not seeking to bond with him, but to get him to sign the necessary adoption papers, which would make Dr. Davis her official step – father. There were some bad feelings which ensued before that meeting between Nancy and her real father. I don't know what was said during their conversation, but what came out of it was the biological father (Kenneth S. Robbins) reluctantly agreed to the adoption. She at this point changed her name to Nancy Davis. Her new step–father (Loyal Davis) was loudly racist and a conservative Republican. These beliefs would be adopted by Nancy, who idolized him, and later shared with her husband to be, Ronald Reagan. Upon moving to Hollywood, she became an actress and a low–level movie starlet. However, she was much more than that, due to her mother's influence in the motion picture business; in other words, she had connections. At this point in reviewing Nancy Davis, a few sentences about her mother would be appropriate. Edith Luckett was a silent film star. In her own career, she rivaled her famous second husband in money making and along the way made influential friends in the movie and theater business. She was also a theatrical actress in New York, and maintained her relationship with this side of the business. Many of her stage acting friends had become major stars in Hollywood: Spencer Tracy, Katherine Hepburn, Lillian Gish and Walter Huston (Uncle Walter to Nancy) to name a few.

Getting back to Nancy's connections. The twenty eight year old small parts actress was first introduced to Reagan in 1949, and evidently developed an interest in him right away. She decided to ask the prominent producer Dore Schary, if he could help set up a more intimate meeting with the actor. Schary's wife Miriam was given the responsibility by her husband to make the arrangements, and she complied by arranging a small dinner party, inviting Ron and Nancy. Just like that; no questions asked. My point is, Nancy knew the right people. I won't go into their courtship, but only to say they were married two years later (1952) in the Little Brown Church in the

Valley in Los Angeles. Nancy was three months pregnant at the time with their first child. Their best man and matron of Honor were the famous actor William Holden and his wife Ardis.

(13)Source: NNDB tracking the entire world – Nancy Reagan – 11/9/09
Nancy Reagan Biography – National First Ladies' Library – 11/9/09
Ronald Reagan Presidential Foundation and Library – 11/9/09

It was through Nancy's tutelage concerning the merits of the Republican Party, which lasted approximately during their courtship time between 1950 to 1952, that Ronald Reagan the former staunch Democrat was now Ronald Reagan, conservative Republican. This wasn't to become official immediately, but the seeds were planted. It wasn't until 1962, when he became a member of the Republican Party, that he devoted himself to party affairs. I don't want to say too much about this transition period: his acting career was on a downward progression, notably in 1954, he was hired to host the General Electric Theater on television, a job he held for eight years. From 1965 to 1966 he hosted and performed on Death

Valley Days, his last acting job.   In January, 1967 he became the 33rd Governor of California, and was re-elected November 3, 1970 for a second four year term as Governor.   Moving right along on January 20, 1981, Reagan was sworn in as the nation's 40th President of the United States.

Now I haven't forgotten the Truman legacy or Reagan's promise to the American people to do a better job than his predecessor Jimmy Carter, which I spoke about earlier, but I'll get to it.   With your indulgence, I would like to digress one more time, and say something about the attempted assassination on his life, March 30, 1981, which falls in the chronological order of his presidency.

What stands out in my mind, while I was researching Reagan for this paper, was Nancy Reagan's strong distrust and dislike for Ron's Vice President George Bush, Sr.   The reason given was the Bush family's opposition to stem cell research, arguing that it could lead to a cure for her husband's Alzheimer's disease.   I agreed with her dislike for Bush, but didn't agree with the reason, entirely.   What I came up with was so shocking, that I had trouble accepting it myself, let alone asking you the reader to believe it.

However, what I'm about to reveal to you is logical and plausible.

First, let me begin with a disturbing statistic, which will set the background for the Reagan shooting. In the span of time between 1963 to 1981, four prominent American leaders were shot: John F. Kennedy, President of the United States – shot and killed in Dallas, TX – 1963; Rev. Martin Luther King, Jr., civil rights activist – shot and killed in Memphis, TN – 1968; Robert F. Kennedy, US Senator and Presidential candidate – shot and killed in Los Angeles, CA – 1968; Ronald W. Reagan, President of the United States – shot and wounded in Washington, DC – 1981. All this shooting of prominent leaders couldn't be a coincidence; there must be a link somewhere. So I took it from there, and tried to logically evaluate it and discover the link. First off, all four men had one trait in common: they were very popular with the American people, and with popularity comes fear and envy. The best intentioned people will fall prey to these evils. We all know, who did the actual shooting of President Reagan; what we don't know is, did the assailant act alone, or was it prearranged from another source?   Being an ex–Marine, security is taught the recruit from the beginning of his training.   To a Marine it is appalling that a shooter would be allowed to get this close to the Chief Executive, where he can get off six rounds, wounding the president, his press secretary and a police officer. The question must be asked, why the potential assassin was allowed to approach the President of the United States with a loaded weapon.   Other questions come to mind: how did the shooter know where the president would be, and that he wouldn't be wearing a bullet proof vest?   The assailant knew too much, and was given too much leeway.   Was the Secret Service that lax in doing their job, or was there a third party involved? Remember Vice President Bush was the Director of the Central Investigation Agency (CIA) 1976 – 1977.   He would be the President of the United States if Reagan was dead, thus he had the motive and a possible means (the CIA) for the attempted assassination.   You already know my distrust of this agency, especially back then.   I can't prove Bush's involvement, and neither could Nancy Reagan.   You know the old saying, "once bitten, twice shy."   She at that point took full control over her husband's schedule, and changed it frequently at the last minute. That's how you do it; stay one step ahead of the enemy; don't let him know where you'll be. She blamed her diversion on astrologer's advice, she took, regarding the best days for the president to travel. Maybe that's true or maybe it isn't, but the fact of the matter is, it worked!

Now back to the Reagan report card and his question: is the American public any better off after the Carter Presidency. Of course I'll ask the question, "after the Reagan Presidency." Let's start off with taxes. Most Americans feel they pay too many taxes. President Reagan decided to cut taxes; for me (a normal guy), it came to about a couple of hundred dollars a year for each cut. Now if I was rich, depending how rich, it would come to about a couple million dollars a year. Since I'm not, the cuts were almost unnoticed. Rather an imbalance between rich and poor, wouldn't you say? However, Reagan was confident, when speaking to the media, explaining the cuts would be effective in stimulating the sagging economy, since the extra money given to the wealthy would trickle down to the average

American, in the form of new business, jobs and so forth. I'm not sure, where Reagan got this idea; perhaps it was part of the Loyal Davis conservative thinking which Nancy imparted to him. In any event it did not work. During an economic slowdown, the rich normally put their money in safe investments such as Government Treasuries, and wait out the bad times, until the economy turns around. That is exactly what took place. However, it wasn't all that bad: I was able to take my wife out to dinner at a nice restaurant every time we had a tax cut. How much of this stimulated the economy, is hard to say, but the old lady did have a wonderful time. That's from the normal person's point of view; from the rich person's point of view, I don't think they did that much.

Reagan always gave speeches about balancing the budget, and like all politicians always blamed the other party for not being able to make ends meet. Back then we had a Democratic Congress. Yet with all his talk, he and the Congress spent money like drunken sailors on leave. This, as you all know, isn't conservative; it is liberal. Kind of makes you think Reagan was both or apolitical. (14) During his two terms as President, the national debt rose from $700 billion to $3 trillion. In order to cover new federal budget deficits, the United States moved from being the world's largest international creditor to the world's largest debtor nation. President Reagan described the new debt as the "greatest disappointment" of his time in office. This was another first for the oldest president: no one of his predecessors ever owed 3 trillion bucks. Reagan, however, wanting the last word, went on to say, that Congress should pass a bill, which mandated the budget must be balanced every year no matter what. He didn't say what government service or department should be cut to accomplish this mandate. Perhaps he had Social Security or Medicare in mind, when he made this suggestion. I present this as a possibility, because during his administration the government went into the FICA funds regularly to pay the day to day bills of running the country. This in time would create a serious shortage of funds, threatening the future of these old age benefits. For a pension type reserve, it is illegal to violate these funds.

(14) Source: Reaganomics, from

Speaking of failures and overspending, this brings me to the Star Wars defense system, dreamed up by the Pentagon, and dubbed Star Wars after the famous science fiction motion picture of the same name. The system, when in place, would have armed war head missiles launched and put into an orbital satellite path. These weapons of mass destruction, as they circle the earth, could be fired on any site, in retaliation for an enemy attack. The devices were mainly directed as a threat to any Communist Bloc country, who had thoughts of a strike on a free world nation. Star Wars was the president's favorite defense commitment, and he put his support to it throughout most of his tenure in office. It cost the taxpayers dearly, and was a good part of the three trillion dollar deficit during his presidency. He got away with it with Congress, because his approval rating with the American people was so high. For the life of me, I can't understand why the rating was so high, since his record in office speaks for itself, but give the man credit for pulling it off. What I do see, is the man used the oldest ploy: create an enemy and scare your constituents with how dangerous this foe is to national security. With the Cold War in place, it was easy to come up with something like the Evil Empire theme, named for the Communist Bloc countries. This brings me back to the Military/Industrial Complex warning of President Eisenhower. How many large government contracts were awarded to big corporations for this never completed Star Wars' defense project, and other defense measures, which came out of the Reagan Administration?

Allow me to explain what a trillion is, so you'll get an idea of the enormity of it: a trillion is one thousand billion and a billion is one thousand million and a million is one thousand, thousand. To raise this kind of money the government must borrow on the open market, competing with other companies. This raises the interest rate and makes investment difficult, since money becomes hard to get. Now as you all know, it cost money to borrow money. The more you borrow, the more you owe. It is no different with the government; as a result the deficit goes up, and the problem festers. More of this will be discussed in The

Supply and Demand chapter.   As of this writing, the only other President, who had a trillion dollar deficit was George Bush Sr.; Reagan's Vice President and successor.   Probably Bush would say he inherited this deficit from his predecessor, or maybe he wouldn't say that.   I'm not quite sure; perhaps he also wanted to run up the debt?   However, that is a paper for another day.

Going from taxes to taxation, President Reagan, along with a Democratic majority Congress, passed The Tax Reform Act of 1986.   The new law increased the taxpayer's annual exemption allowance for each dependent from $1,080 to $1,900.   That's the good part of it; the bad part was, it did away with most tax deductions, which the average American worker could take, such as sales tax, medical costs, business expenses, loan interest, etc.   The only other exemptions that remained were home mortgage interest and charitable contributions.   Being just an ordinary person, depending on exemptions to lower my taxes, it resulted in raising them on top of already high taxes.   No one in the government told us they would be higher; we had to find this out for ourselves, since the change over to the new system was done gradually over a three year period. I'm not sure how the rich fit into the new plan; I was only worrying about myself at the time. However, if I was a betting man, I would bet on the rich coming out ahead in all this, especially when you look at the capital gains tax reductions in the new law. I believe it is duly noted that the average person seldom has capital gains.

(1) Under the new tax regulations, the capital gains tax rates were generally reduced across the board. These applied to long term capital gains, gains on hobbies and real estate, and under the five year rule of investments gains over five years. Like all tax laws, they are so complicated, it would take several pages of, "if this – then that," breakdown of exactly what they are. I'll spare you the details in this paper, and suggest, you consult some of the literature on the subject from the IRS. At the same time, let me warn you the capital gains taxes change from one administration to another, generally speaking. What becomes fair between the two types of tax payers (rich versus poor) is up for debate, depending on which side of the fence you're standing: Democrats or Republicans. What is of paramount importance with any taxation is, it

must give consideration to the citizens, who live from one paycheck to another; that they shouldn't be overtaxed. From the Reagan/Congress tax reform came a dangerous possibility of this happening. It certainly didn't help the nation's economy, nor did it do anything about the country's deficit.

(1)Source: The World Almanac and Book of Facts 1999

Reagan had a different approach to economics than his predecessor. As I previously mentioned, he believed in supply side economics, which isn't anything new theoretically speaking, especially to the Republican Party and his father-in-law Loyal Davis. This concept passed on to him through Nancy. Briefly, it espouses the government, in its policy towards business, should err on the side of the suppliers, who reinvest in the economy and rejuvenate it with business dealings and innovative merchandising ideas. This in turn provides jobs, which provides further stimulus to the nation's economy. I went over this before, but it bears retelling, since it previews Reagan's belief in largeness in industries. To quote him, "bigness isn't necessarily badness." Incorrect English, I know, but it got his point over to the American public. What he was preparing the country for was, his administration wasn't going to enforce the Anti-Trust Laws. This started a trend in business, which was and is still scary. Enormous buyouts began to occur unprecedented in the nation's history, which spread all over the world like a bad disease. Let me explain the concept of doing this, so you won't think this is total madness. The idea goes something like this: as companies buy out their competition they eliminate duplication of effort, thereby saving the new combined company money. For example, two companies have two accounting departments; when the companies merge, they need only one department, and can cut the overall staff substantially, and so forth and so on throughout the entire combined organization. The savings at that point can be passed on to the consumer in the form of less expensive products or services. Again the term "trickledown theory" applies: whatever savings realized are passed down to the public. But, is this in fact what happens?

Allow me to explain in more detail. A large corporation decides: since we have more demand for 'A' machines, we will need a new plant to meet the demand requirements. With Reaganomics there is no need to do this; simply go into the stock market and gain control through a corporate buy out of 'X' company stock, who also makes 'A' machines. And just that simple the large company has its' plant(s) to meet the extra demand. However, it isn't that simple. The buying of a company in order to buy a competing company requires taking out heavy loans. In order to help pay them off, they have to go into their new acquisition, and start cutting back on company expenses, and company expenses usually translates into cutting back the number of employees, who are on the payroll. This usually affects productivity, and the service to customers. The new combined organization is less capable of competing in the overall world market. Then, of course, unemployment becomes an issue. To examine this a little closer: the employees cut are usually the older more experienced ones, who through years of experience have developed skills in doing their jobs. They go to work every day; are loyal to the firm; take care of their customers, and make a quality product. However, over the years, their salaries have grown, and as such, they have become layoff targets for the new owners. Moving on, the new owners hire a systems analyst to come in and look over the situation. These analysts don't know the nature of the company's work they are evaluating, nor do they care about the employees or in developing a better way of using them. They aren't that creative. They rely on out-sourcing, mandatory retirement or any devious method of getting rid of people, especially older employees. This results in sudden surges of unemployment throughout the nation, as these buyouts take place. It appears to be a win, win position for large companies, because they are getting rid of older employees, who have pensions, health care insurance, accumulated vacation, sick time and other expenses which younger workers don't have. On paper it looks better, since it cuts administrative expense, which gives the buyout company a better profit and loss picture for now, and increases their ability to pay off debt.

This is right out of the Loyal Davis play book, so to speak. It takes away people from the equation of the American Empire. Do this and you won't have an Empire. The rich have a tendency to do that; they live an isolated life on some vast ranch somewhere, where no one can find them or interact with them. You know the old saying coined by Marie Antoinette, "give them cake." People, not only make up Empires, they also make up markets. Markets make the world go round. Take away their spending power, and the market suffers. Large empires have been brought to their knees because of a selfish disregard for people. Check out the British Empire, as an example. They diminished their middle class with the same Loyal Davis conservative thinking, and are at the point of not being able to restore it, even though they try. Once the damage is done, it isn't easy to get it back. Oh, one more thing, is the product or service any less expensive as suggested it would be, because of the 'bigness' theory? You tell me. What does drive the cost of goods and services down is competition; not eliminating competition.

As I alluded to before, history has a way of judging us all, and it has indeed judged Ronald Reagan on his 'bigness' acceptance, as well as other policies of his. Let's examine what has happened as a result of the Reagan/Davis 'bigness' theory.   (2)In 2002 an alarming number of corporate scandals occurred beginning with Enron, when the nation's largest energy trader, filed for bankruptcy, December, 2001.   This was the result of them being under federal investigation for hiding debt and misrepresenting earnings.   The company used complicated off-the-balance-sheet partnerships to inflate profits by as much as $600 million.   Enron's fall had a strong impact on the economy, as well as leaving their employees without their retirement funds.   The auditing and accounting firm of Arthur Anderson, who worked for Enron, also went under, after they destroyed critical documents which supported the federal charges. WorldCom (July, 2002), was the country's second-largest firm to go bankrupt in the nation's history, after they admitted to falsifying their accounting books.   Among other companies, who were also placed under investigation for crooked accounting and other fraudulent misadventures were Tyco, Qwest, Global Crossing, ImClone, and Adelphia.   In addition to this, were stories of extravagantly paid CEO's, who went overboard with their personal perks and enrichment with a total disregard for their employees.   These leaders displayed arrogance, greed and a defiance toward the nation's laws and the mission of their company. Yes, 'bigness' is badness. There is more of the same, going on in many large firms. My partner and I are growing weary of telling them. Let it suffice that the Reagan legacy in regard to big business has hurt the nation immensely and the American people as well. Not to forget harming competition, which is the driving force of our free enterprise system.

(2)Source: TIME Almanac 2003

Very quietly during the Reagan Administration the American Labor Unions have gone away; not completely, but their membership has declined. Until now they represent only eleven percent of the working force. Can you blame Reagan for this? I like to believe that you can. The buck has to stop somewhere, and like President Truman, I believe it stops with the President of the United States. He was in charge of the Attorney General's office wasn't he, and isn't it the responsibility of that office to prosecute any infractions of the law? Well they did not. Union membership during the Reagan time in office went from 22% to 16% of the labor force.

Source: Bureau of Labor Statistics, US Department of Labor, from The World Almanac and Book of Facts 1999.

Labor Unions in the United States have been legal since 1840. For a company to fire someone, who is trying to organize a labor union in a factory or home office of that company is illegal. Let's evaluate it from a closer look. A corporation decides they have to retool in order to be more competitive. Usually they don't update the plant, which has been in existence for a number of years. Instead, they build at another site, perhaps hundreds or thousands of miles away. Why? They give all sorts of reasons, and of course it is their prerogative to do this. However, asking why is a good question. Is this an attempt to escape the unions? It seems that way, since the unions rarely go with them to the new site. If someone dares try establishing a trade union in the new plant/office, that person will be out of there before he knows what hit him. Isn't that illegal? President Reagan didn't think so, and neither did any of the judges, who tried the cases. So where does that leave the unions? In a bad place; they now represent about 11% of the nation's workers. They represent them from a very weak position, since the law enforcement is no longer on their side. Now I'm not arguing in behalf of the trade unions. It's hard to do that in light of all the scandal, deviant behavior and underworld connections they were associated with back in the 1940's and 1950's. However, Reagan and the conservatives forgot one important fact, when they destroyed them: who or what is going to replace them? As it now stands, the American worker is on his own going up against mega-sized corporations. Their jobs aren't protected, nor do they have any long term prospective with an organization, which could lead to a decent pension in their old age or health care insurance. A company can lay off or fire any employee, anytime they want to do it for any reason. Hence, the average worker in his country will lose his position several times during his/her career, and quite possibly will need to be retrained almost as many times. Retrained, by the way, at their own expense.

Reagan's role in ending the Cold War is debatable in my mind, since I have difficulty understanding, what he did to end it. My partner and I read everything available on the subject, and researched it as fully as our time would allow. Our conclusion was no one or no individual(s) ended the Cold War; it ended itself. Reagan, in our minds, used the Soviet Union and Communism as a scapegoat to divert attention away from his own failures as president of this nation, and he had many. He dubbed them the "Evil Empire," sounding much like a movie theme: the USA are the good guys, and the USSR are the baddies. Get real will you; what was happening in the world wasn't a second rate movie plot. It was weapons of mass destruction being used by two power hungry empires, who were threatening to blow up each other or possibly the world. In time, if we all survived, one power or the other would outlast the other; as it turned out the USA would be that power. The Viet Nam War, which the USSR funded from the Communist side, left that power on the ropes economically. Reagan and his aides must have been aware of this fact, as we were, and used it to his advantage. Or perhaps we are giving him too much credit. The Evil Empire was even buying wheat from the USA. What kind of a threatening power can it be, which can't even feed their own people? In time, a fool would concede, the Soviet Union was doomed to fail.

However, Reagan did take advantage of the Communist threat, and held it over the American peoples' heads. He rarely let an opportunity go by without reminding them what a menace communism was to mankind and the Free World. The Great Communicator (as Reagan was called) was, as his nickname implied, communicating, but to whom, and was it doing any good. (13)Nancy Reagan didn't feel her husband was getting anywhere with all this uncomplimentary dialogue aimed at communism, and made her views known to her husband and the administration. Not a First Lady to interfere with State Department issues, she stepped out of this role briefly to promote the idea of the President forming a personal relationship with the new Soviet President Mikhail Gorbachev, when he assumed power in 1985. Her reasoning: "simply because it made no sense that the two leaders were not at least in open dialogue with each other." The resulting amity between the two, and then political negotiations, brought about the INF Treaty in 1987, which called for a mutual destruction of intermediate range nuclear missiles. The treaty turned out to be the most significant accomplishment of the Reagan Administration, and was considered by many as an important step in ending the Soviet communism. (Not the writer's opinion). Nancy in seeing this through, did so in spite of the fact that she underwent breast cancer surgery, soon after the death of her mother.

(13)Source: Nancy Reagan Biography: National First Ladies' Library, 11/9/09 – Internet

Out of Hitler's Germany in the nineteen thirties came an automobile, which would later in the post war Germany revolutionize the car industry. They named it the Volkswagen or the people's car. Hitler's auto was a small vehicle with an air cooled engine, which ran on little gas, and was easy to park and drive as well as inexpensive to overhaul. It gave Germany dependable transportation for the masses. The company survived the Second World War and went international in the early sixties, at which time I bought one new. The car served me and my family (wife and children) for over twelve years, getting us to where we had to go inexpensively.

The auto was everything the creators wanted it to be, but like everything it had its' faults. One was it came out second best in a fender bender or highway accident, behind the larger American cars. This eventually was what made me give up on it, as the roads became more crowded with aggressive drivers, driving faster more powerful cars. However, the auto had its' effect on American markets by giving birth to the gas efficient compact auto, especially during the gas crunch of the late nineteen seventies. This style car is no longer made in its' original form, but the Volkswagen Company has made a mark in the international market with other styles of automobiles.

Ronald Reagan's car on the other hand was almost the opposite of the VW or Beetle, as people affectionately called it. The Reagan car was the SUV or Sport Utility Vehicle. It was and is big and boxy, and expensive to drive, especially with gas consumption; hard to park and operate in normal road conditions; complicated to overhaul and its' parts, being larger, are more costly. The thing it had in common with the VW was both vehicles were dangerous to their drivers on the open road.   The VW, with the gas tank in the front, made it a potential danger in a front end collision, since it gave the operator little protection in a headlong collision and a flammable threat from the fuel igniting on impact.   As big as the 'off-the-road' SUV's were, one would think they would be more stable on the open highway.   However, this wasn't so, since they were top heavy causing them to roll over, when hit by another vehicle. Additionally their weight in the back and relatively narrow wheel base, caused fishtailing at high speeds under certain road conditions.   This was realized by the previous administration (Carter), who did a number of studies on the matter, and although never completed, they gathered enough information to be suspect of the vehicle's safety. Regardless of their findings, Ronald Reagan's people rewrote the paper drafted on the vehicle's safety, stating otherwise.   The new President even went so far as to go on television, defending how these autos were built insisting the American public was safe riding in them.   Without the benefit of an investigation or study, he insisted American car manufacturers were the best auto makers in the world, and most certainly wouldn't deceive the

American people, placing them in an unsafe vehicle. This was sadly wrong; it resulted in a higher percentage of deaths and mutilations of American motorists over the years because both drivers of the SUV's and those in normal cars collided with these larger vehicles. As a result of class action and single law suits against the six major automobile manufacturers for making unsafe vehicles, this mistake in judgment is now being rectified to make SUV's safer; very much in accord with the previous suggestions of the Carter administration. I'll have more to report on the SUV menace in the next chapter on road safety.

Now to conclude this topic, my partner and I can only come to one inference about President Reagan's hasty decision on SUV safety. He was prompted by money and big business; not human lives and safety. Ignorance was no excuse here; he should have done his homework before recommending the SUV to the American public. He was the President of the United States. Remember President Truman's advice about the office: "the buck stops here." The people trusted him; he was their leader, and they paid and are still paying a terrible price for listening to him. Their lives and safety and that of their children are at stake here.

Iran/Contra Scandal:

Reagan had a scandal in his administration, but he didn't know about it, until everybody else found out about it. President of the United States and he didn't know what people under him were doing with millions of dollars of taxpayers' money. Hard to believe, but that's what was accepted by Congress and the American people. It was called the Iran/Contra Scandal, which seemed minor compared to the SUV Reagan deception, and other mistakes in his presidency. It was revealed in the latter part of 1986. The plan was to send arms to Iran; exchanging arms for hostages. Oliver North, a Colonel in the United States Marine Corps was the fall guy in all this. In his testimony before a congressional inquiry, he informed Congress that higher officials approved his secret Iran/Contra operations. Admiral John M. Poindexter (North's boss), and former National Security Adviser, later testified he authorized use of Iran arms sale profits to aid the Contras – the second patsy in the scandal. Next on the list, Secretary of State George P. Shultz testified he was deceived repeatedly on the Iran–Contra affair. Right up the line, Defense Secretary Casper W. Weinberger told Congress of official deception and intrigue. Then the buck finally stopped. Reagan advised that Iran/Contras arms policy went astray, and accepted full responsibility.

The above is essentially the Iran/Contras scandal in a nutshell, which to me appears rather tame next to; "not enforcing the Anti -Trust Laws" as well as the SUV's/Reagan endorsement scandals. What did come out of the Iran/Contra affair, which attracted our attention, was a report by a presidential commission released in February, 1987, showing Reagan, when questioned about the incident, was confused and uniformed, and concluded that his relaxed administrative style had kept him from controlling those under him. Of course he was relaxed, because his mind couldn't comprehend the seriousness of the moment, since it was influenced by a disease.

The terms "confused" and "uniformed" (perhaps memory loss) were expressions familiar to me in describing my mother's condition, because she too suffered from Alzheimer's disease. She had this terrible disorder for about ten years; her brilliant mind steadily declined over that period, until she didn't know, who I was. I speak of the ailment from personal experience. I believe Nancy knew her husband had this disorder, while still in office. Ronald Reagan himself gave hint to this in his 1990 Autobiography, when he wrote, "Although she never brought it up, I think Nancy would have preferred that I not run for reelection, in 1984. But I never doubted I would." Who was better qualified to suspect Reagan's illness that his wife of fifty years. She lived with him every day, and knew his weaknesses. She should have said something to him.

Alzheimer's disease doesn't belong in the Oval Office. This is the purpose of the Vice President: to take over the Presidency, when the President is unable to fulfill his duties to the country. We strongly feel Reagan was in this position at that time. He admitted he didn't know about the diversion of funds for the Iran/Contras affair. I suppose he didn't; he didn't remember. You can be sure he did approve it. That kind of money can only be obtained through the signature of the President of the United States. Oliver North revealed this to the news media, when questioned;

his answer, "do you think a bird Colonel (referring to himself) can order up all this equipment, and spend that kind of money without approval from high up? Good question, Oliver: of course not. Alzheimer Disease is a progressive, degenerative disorder of the brain, where brain cells die, and are not replaced. The disease is the most common form of a dementia, characterized by memory loss, thinking process disruption, and abnormal behavior. The progression rate of the disease from its onset of symptoms ranges from 3 to 20 years; the average is eight years.   If my math is correct, the beginning symptoms of the disease would have affected President Reagan somewhere in his second term in office. He was diagnosed with it in 1994; his last year in office was 1989.

Warning signs: memory loss which affects job performance, use of inappropriate words when communicating, disorientation to time and place, and problems with abstract thinking. Additionally, there may be rapid changes in mood or behavior and prolonged loss of initiative. Of the twelve warning signs listed in my source material, I've reduced them to the ones I felt President Reagan showed me in his second term of office. If I am correct in my appraisal of the man, you may want to know, who did run the country during this time? It is our opinion that Nancy Reagan took charge more and more during this period and with the help of trusted aides filled in the blank spaces in Reagan's thinking and behavior, and led the country. Any other first Lady, we feel, wouldn't be capable of this; Nancy Reagan wasn't just any First Lady. She was intelligent and capable of grabbing the bull by the horns, so to speak, and taking charge behind the scenes in her leadership. Ronald Reagan was quite fortunate to have her for his wife. She, we believe, got him through this time in office, without it being known.

(1)Source: Alzheimer Association, Chicago, IL, found in the World Almanac and Book of Facts 1999.

Now we're not attempting to minimize Reagan's fault in the Iran/Contra's affair. The man broke the law of this nation, whether he was aware of it or not, and should be held accountable, but wasn't. As mentioned before this scandal seems to be the least of what Reagan did to my country. Unchecked "bigness" in corporate business has in the twenty first century brought America to its' knees economically. People are losing their homes, cars and jobs as a result. Management of these large corporations have come under unscrupulous CEO's, who stole from the company they represented, and covered up for their poor management with falsified accounting practices. Yes the "bigness" that Ronald Reagan lauded as being good, wasn't, and we as a nation are paying a terrible price for his error in judgment. Theodore Roosevelt, our twenty–sixth President and also a conservative Republican, realized this. He went up against the trusts and monopolies at every turn in his administration. This same flaw in the American economic system has been going on in the early 20th century since Roosevelt. He felt nothing in this nation should be stronger than the office of the President. When this happens, the people no longer have representation in its power. A nation, such as the United States, can't have free enterprise, when whole industries are controlled by one or few organizations. It takes away incentive and the normal function of the markets they serve.

Reagan was also appalled with Labor

Unions, and so he should be. Their record of unfair and unlawful practices speaks for itself. However, in his judgment, he didn't give thought, to who would replace them as a spokesman for the American worker. Today the average American worker is at the mercy of large impersonal corporations, who employ an army of lawyers and human resource specialists to deal with the company's most important resource – their employees. The idea of a steady job is a thing of the past. With this goes the idea of long term economic investing from the American labor force. This is a great loss for the nation's economy, and banking system as well.

In order to adapt to the loss of the steady job, many American families have evolved into two income families. Even with two incomes, the family is stretched to its' financial limits to make ends meet. The family relationship is likewise stretched with absentee mothers leaving their children to an empty house, when they come home from school. The country will be affected by this as these children grow up and take over the nation. Since their upbringing will lack close parental training, morality and the conviction to do the right thing will also be compromised. God only knows, where this will take America.

Long term relationships between a company and their employees will no longer exist. This detachment will take the heart and soul out of the firm because employees will react accordingly with less than satisfactory effort on behalf of the customers. Computers can't do everything; without good employees behind them, they are worthless. You know the old saying, "garbage in, garbage out." If companies believe these machines can effectively replace people, they are in for a big disappointment. Good performance always comes down to good employees.

What did Ronald Reagan do for the forgotten peoples of this land to make their lives better? What I'm referring to by the term "forgotten peoples" is our population's senior citizens or people over fifty five years old. First off, mandatory early retirement came out of his administration, fueled by outsourcing and sending jobs overseas. This was done with disregard for the quality of the older employees' job performance. During Reagan's administration, the Federal Treasury had to go into the FICA funds, since the President ran the country on poor monetary policy, and record deficit spending. This tapping of FICA reserves (supposedly protected) threatened the very existence of Medicare and Social Security.

I wish with all my heart that the Iran/Contra scandal was the only wrong Ronald Reagan did in his eight years in office. We, as a nation and hardworking people, would be far better off, if that were true. Terrorists and thugs like the Iran hostage takers and the Contras come and go, but the reckless policies of the Reagan Administration will be with American citizens for a long time, doing untold damage to their lifestyles, and the generations to come. We buried Ronald Reagan yesterday, and with him we buried many of our rights and freedoms. He was popular with the people, and they listened to him. Like the Pied Piper of Hamelin, he led America with his charming magical talk; like a flute, it played on and on, until the average citizen couldn't see, what he was doing to them. His magical talk is now silenced, and hopefully the folly of his policies will come to light. Definitely the consequences of them have.

END OF: REAGAN

ROAD SAFETY

It was a sunny June day only a few years ago, when my wife and I came across the accident. We were coming back from visiting friends in College Park, PA, along the Pennsylvania Turnpike, somewhere near the city of Reading. The drive up to that point was somewhat uneventful, for which we were grateful. We were looking forward to arriving home safely, having a small dinner and relaxing. Every person who desires to drive an SUV should see a major accident involving one before buying this vehicle. It is gruesome, something a horror movie can't quite picture. Indeed real life is more realistic and captures in detail what any man's imagination can't do. Immediately my wife and I knew what had happened, even though it wasn't at first apparent. There was a sudden shock and silence, which came over the road, which I can't quite explain, as if life and the noise of the open road had come to a stop. In a sense it did. Cars were parked along the shoulder of the highway, and their drivers were searching for something, looking dazed.   Then we saw what they were looking at; trying to understand what had happened.   They couldn't understand it, because they never saw it before.   To them an auto accident was just a statistic: so many died every year; so many were mutilated, etc.   This sort of disaster happens without explanation.   You have to see it to comprehend what it is.   This is what my wife and I, and the others saw, up front and ugly.

Glass and blood surrounded two young teenaged women, who lay unconscious on the road, apparently in shock, going in and out of consciousness, and also apparently in a great deal of pain, which was evidenced from their moans and shivering, as they briefly came to and then lapsed back to the relief of unconsciousness.   My wife, a Registered Nurse asked me to pull over, which I did unhesitatingly.   We hurriedly made our way back through the crowded scene of people, who were somewhat dazed, and trying to see how they could help.   My wife familiar with such events, had more of a take charge approach as she neared the accident site.   She immediately addressed the motorists, who were hovering over the stricken young women, identifying herself and her professional licensing. Various witnesses were talking at the same time to themselves and to us. What we could get out of their information was sketchy but soon understandable. The young man driving the SUV, now smashed solidly into the three foot metal guard rail, and had deliberately rear ended a small compact car, knocking it over the guard rail into the heavy bush area which bordered the road. The small car, upon impact, sailed in mid-air, until a large tree ended its' flight, where it dropped, and found its' rest. Being an ex-Marine, I remember their training in how to deal with a wounded buddy: immediately treat for shock; make the victim as warm as possible. Going back to the SUV, I found some blankets on its' back tailgate, which had sprung open upon impact. I covered the women with them, and while I was doing this, my wife went through the brush to see what she could do for the driver of the compact car.

When I caught up with her, she was returning from the compact car site. Her face was pale from what she saw. In all her experience in seeing accident victims in the Emergency Room of the hospital, she never saw anything this gruesome. I wanted to go back, and see if I could do anything for him. She asked me not to: "there is nothing you can do for him; I couldn't perform CPR on him; his body is so badly twisted out of shape, and there is so much blood and debris. Please, don't go back there; stay with me." We returned to the highway: there leaning against the guardrail was the driver of the SUV. Obviously he was a teenager; tall and gaunt looking; now dazed; face covered with blood, and he had wet himself. Otherwise he was able to stand, and in the best condition of all five victims.

Further down the shoulders of the highway, we found the fifth victim, hardly noticeable; lying beyond the guardrail in a clump of bushes, where he was thrown during the impact. My wife examined him, and found, although unconscious, he was breathing quite normally, and the bleeding on his body was rather superficial and not life threatening. He would die five days later of internal complications from the collision. At that point the ambulance and the police were beginning to arrive. Before we left a woman and her two sons struck up a conversation with us. She witnessed the accident. Her sons were sleeping, when it happened. "He deliberately rear–ended the smaller car," she told us. "I saw the whole thing; I'm going to tell the police, what he did." I congratulated her on what she was going to do, but somehow I felt the police wouldn't do anything about it. They didn't. It would go down as just another auto accident.

Here's what the evening news reported about the collision. The children in the SUV, were just graduated from high school, and the night before went to their Senior Prom. They were returning from some next day celebration of the event. The driver and his best friend had their dates with them; none of them were seat belted in. Nothing was said about the police pressing charges against the driver. I was right. The news people withheld the name of the compact car driver, since his next of kin wasn't yet notified. The only other news worthy report on the incident came five days later, when the driver's best friend had been rushed to the hospital with internal complications from the accident, which that day took his life.

I'll go over the dangers of the SUV further

on in this paper, but first I would like to address the most dangerous driver on the highway: the under 25 year old driver.   To do that, the question 'why' should be asked; why should this group be the most dangerous, and if this is so, what can be done to bring them under control? The insurance companies charge the highest premiums to insure them, and raise their rates according to each accident they have. Does that stop them? No. What would help? Well for starters, mandatory Driver's Education for every teen learning to drive. To have their parents teach them is pure folly; they don't know how to drive a car. In simple terms these children are being taught by fools, who break the law every time they operate a car: speeding, going through yield and stop signs, red lights, etc., bullying other motorists on the road, driving too close, not wearing seat belts. It sounds like the signs posted along the road warning motorists about these infractions. As part of the education, teens should see films and pictures of what my wife and I saw on the Pennsylvania turnpike. You know the old saying, "one picture is worth a thousand words." If these kids are going to play the game of driving on hazardous roads, they should know the consequences of their actions. Oh, you say that is going to scare them, and cause them mental anguish. I hope so. What is better, mental anguish or death and mutilation from car crashes? Mental anguish can be dealt with; death and mutilation are forever.

(15) My partner likes statistics to back up our argument, so to honor his wishes, I would like to review the car crash in question, and see how it stacks up with four major statistics furnished me by the Allstate Motor Club. The company provides road service in the event of a road mishap, so they deal with this problem on a regular basis. The following are their annual numbers on nationwide accident statistics and totals.

Fatalities in Traffic Crashes	42,642
Injured in Traffic Crashes	2,575,000
Alcohol Related Deaths	17,602
Speeding Related Deaths	13,543

(15)Source: National Highway Traffic Safety Administration, 2006 data.

In the one accident, we witnessed, caused by the teen SUV driver, he killed two people, and seriously injured three, including himself. The witness told me, he was speeding and deliberately struck the compact car. The latter suggests he was driving under the influence of either drugs or alcohol (or possibly hung-over from the night before), which explains his bizarre driving. So our young man was at fault for and added to all of the above statistics. I have no way of knowing if the teen in question had driver's education courses. Would it have made a difference in his driving behavior? I don't know. Would driver's education make a difference in generally lowering the above statistics? I would say definitely, yes; substantially!

To support the above conclusions, I have one more statistic to add concerning young people driving on the open road, which was provided by 2009 SafeCarGuide.com, Inc. The number one cause of death and injury for young people ages 5 to 27 in America was traffic collisions.

The next deterrent to lowering road collisions would be the police. My wife and I drove over a hundred turnpike miles on the accident day, and didn't see a police car in all that time. Also it took an inordinate amount of time for the police to arrive at the collision site. Our estimate was about a half an hour or possibly longer. Where are the police? They know the statistics, as well as I know them. Why aren't they out on the highway enforcing the law? When I asked (various policemen I interviewed on the subject), they gave me two reasons: one they don't have the manpower, and two the laws have changed making an arrest difficult without a witness, willing to go into court, if a situation arises. I always thought a ticket is a ticket, and all the arresting officer has to do is testify in court, if an appeal is made. Why would this change? Is it a law, or is it how a judge would interpret it? The criterion is bad anyway you look at it. Law or no law, the police should still make a presence on the open road. The battle is there, not behind a desk somewhere or wherever they go.

Now I'm talking about the police here. The police, who should serve the people, and defend them from the criminal element. Why should they do that? Well it's their duty. True, but why should they do their duty? Many in the American Empire don't. Why should they? There is a pragmatic reason: if they don't, the American people might get the idea, they don't need them anymore. But, you say, "what can we do without police?" Maybe we can do without some of them; especially since they aren't doing anything, which I can see. Why not cut the police force substantially, and hire security guards to do the hands-on duty, the police aren't handling. Can't be done? It can: in Philadelphia SEPTA has their own security guards, and Drexel University is in the process of organizing their own police force to protect their students and teachers. The latter has had so many robberies against their students i.e. breaking and entering and car break-ins, they felt compelled to make this move. I believe prominent universities, like Drexel, will be getting into the security business more and more. They have the money to afford it, and, of course, they have an obligation toward the safety and well-being of their faculty and student body. Without these two, the college is out of business. If these two organizations, I've mentioned, can do this, why can't a community do the same? The security company can be evaluated every year(s) by the mayor's office or township commissioners (both elected officials), and fired if they aren't doing the job, in favor of another security firm. Presently the community can't fire the police, and they know it.

Now, I'm not saying to do without the police altogether. Treat them like any other administrative body, and insist they cooperate with the security force. It's just an idea of mine. Has anybody come up with a better plan on how to handle the problem? One other advantage of hired security guards is in fighting corruption, which has a tendency to seep into a stand-pat police force. Remember, Americans are very innovative in dealing with a problem. Give them an idea, which I am doing, and you'd be surprised at what they can do with it.

The third deterrent to road hazards is the automotive manufacturers. Why should they make a vehicle, which is unsafe? These people are auto makers. They know, as well as I do that the SUV, used to transport passengers on the open road is unsafe for it's passengers and the passengers of the normal cars they collide with in the event of a crash.   Knowing this, they continue to produce and sell them, without a disclaimer warning to buyers. Why should a President of the United States appear before the American public on television, insisting that the SUV is safe, when he knows it isn't (refer to the Reagan chapter for more data)? Why should such a vehicle have the capacity to go as fast as 140 miles per hour, knowing there will be people driving them, who are irresponsible and unqualified to handle these vehicles? Is money that important to the suppliers? Apparently it is.

(16) To substantiate our opening statement in the chapter, we have tapped into an information data base provided by the Newsome Law Firm. Our thanks go out to them and their efforts to inform the public of the SUV hazard. In their studies concerning vehicle rollovers, they found that SUV's are more susceptible to rollovers than normal cars. Briefly, a rollover is when the vehicle flips over on its' side or roof; the mishap often causes severe injury, property damage, vehicle damage, and death.

An SUV will rollover for a number of reasons; the most prevalent one is turning too fast. Physics will confirm this; notably, for instance the top heavy nature of the vehicle and its' center of mass being higher, combined with the pressures of inertia and gravity going against the wheels.

Other vehicles can also rollover under certain conditions such as, collisions, tipping and rough terrain, just as SUV's, but despite improvements in the past few years, this vehicle is still at greater risk of rollover in an accident. Another factor in rollover with the SUV is speed: due to their high center of mass, the vehicle's stability is compromised, meaning that almost any collision at high speed can result in a rollover.

To make matters worse, the SUV in order to provide more space inside the cab, is built without a roll cage. This is a safety device, which protects the passenger(s), since the roof and sides of the SUV, because of its' weight, collapse under a rollover condition. The cage would give a protective brace to the cab area, limiting the number of fatalities and more serious injuries, especially to the head. This rollover crushing factor can also hinder the passenger(s) and driver escaping the damaged vehicle, since the top, doors and window frames most likely will be crushed in the event. If a fire occurs, they can be burned alive. Lastly, SUV collisions can cause ejections into traffic, if the passengers aren't seat belted in, which was earlier reported in the accident my wife and I witnessed. This is caused by the sheer force of the larger engine capacity.

The statistics are even more alarming. The SUV is 75% more likely than a regular car to be involved in a rollover incident. In the year 2000, over 10,000 people died due to SUV rollover traffic accidents. Sixty two percent of SUV fatalities happened because of a rollover. Rollovers are extremely dangerous: only 3% of all traffic accidents resulted in this, but they were responsible for 33% of the fatalities that year.

(17) If the above statistics concerning the SUV road dangers to the occupants, is disturbing, then what they do to regular car occupants in a collision is much more disturbing. Consider this, four wheel drive SUV's and pick-up trucks were designed to be driven for hauling and off-road purposes.   For open road transportation of humans, they are at a disadvantage, lacking maneuverability and handling dexterity of passenger cars or minivans. As previously mentioned the SUV and pick-up trucks, are four times more likely to roll over than regular cars in high speed maneuvers. This is the result of differences in vehicle weight (mass), height, and

front end size of the larger vehicles. In a SUV–to–car collision, the passengers of the car are six times more likely to be killed, when compared to car–to–car collisions. The passengers in the SUV may be safer, but they put others in the smaller vehicles at a greater risk. Apparently Americans don't care about killing other Americans, and the auto manufacturers don't care either. In their ignorance and devotion to the SUV fad, they don't even know what happened, when they themselves become victims of an SUV collision, and how it all came about. They call it fate, but it isn't that; it is love of money over human life. It has become acceptable, because it is the American style.

Source: (16) Copyrighted 2009 SafeCarGuide.com, Inc., a coachbuilt.com affiliate. (17) SUV Rollover, Statistics, sponsored by the Newsome Law Firm, Orlando, Florida, who represents consumers injured by defective products.

This brings us to the end of ROAD SAFETY. In reading the chapter you have become educated on what is happening to drivers and their families on the open road. The good news is there is technology available to put a serious dent into the deaths and body mutilations caused by traffic mishaps. The bad news is you, the public, must want the changes necessary to bring safety into your habits and lifestyle. Do you? Don't answer that too quickly. Think a little about our question; perhaps human life and safety aren't that important to you. Are they? Are you willing to make sacrifices for safety's sake? Maybe you're not; if that's so, then my partner and I have gone as far as we can on the subject, and can end it right here. If, on the other hand, you are an optimist and a person of high moral standards, you will insist that the human creature is more likely to do the right thing, and will, if solutions are presented, and clearly explained. With that assumption in our perspective, we will attempt to do so. Keep in mind these solutions are available, if you want them.

To begin, we are going to ask you some questions. You don't have to answer them; this is a book, not a questionnaire. You do have to answer them in your heart, because there is a lot at stake here.

..Are you willing to give up talking on the

cell phone, while driving your car? The phone's signals can be blocked in the driver's seat.

..Are you willing to go slower in your car? A governor can be put on the engine to keep it from going past a certain speed. The same can be done by adding a chip to the ignition key.

..Are you willing to have a sensor device on your vehicle, which reduces engine speed, when your auto is getting too close to another vehicle? It can be done.

..Are you willing to have a roll cage or other similar heavy metal apparatus added to your SUV vehicle to protect the passenger cab in the event of a rollover? This will limit space and add to the weight of the auto.

Battering rams can also be added front and back to the conventional car. Of course they aren't attractive, but they even the playing field going up against the larger SUVs and pick-up trucks.

..And speaking of SUV's, are you willing to give them up altogether? The old fashioned station wagon can replace them. This vehicle is safer in itself and in a car-to-car collision. It can also store more. You won't need a rack on top of it, when you're going to the shore, and it is easier to park. It should also save on gas, since it is aerodynamically better designed. Additionally, it is a car made for the open road and has better handling ability at higher speed, and hence more resistance to rollovers.

..Are you willing to pay extra taxes to the school system in your community to support driver's education in the high schools?

..Are you willing to have electronic devices strategically situated on highways, where the accident rate is high, which will automatically ticket the speeder, since the police don't have the manpower to bring this law breaking under control?

..Are you willing to support legislation which will raise the age limit of the new driver to eighteen years old? If the legal age (adulthood) is eighteen, then why isn't it the same for drivers? Those two years would add a lot of maturity to the average teenager, which might save his life and the lives of his passengers. Would it kill you (no pun intended) as a parent to drive him around during this time? You may get to know each other better; you know, quality time together.

End of ROAD SAFETY

CRIME

It stands to reason, if the victim of a crime in the American Empire has no rights, then the rights must go somewhere. It takes little thought to conclude they must go to the criminal, so to evaluate why this is so, one must evaluate the criminal. This will be the purpose of the chapter. My partner and I have concluded, a story about a mutual friend of a friend may well serve this purpose. We will exclude their names, for privacy reasons, since they are not necessary to the content. They may well be embarrassed due to their foolish behavior in dealing with the situation.

This is our story. The old man loved his grandchildren. Being retired he had time to devote to them, and when his daughter came to him to baby sit her youngest, while she worked at the local hospital, he was happy to do it. There was a regimen his daughter had with the running of the household and getting the oldest children off to school in the morning. This included feeding the baby, and getting her ready for her morning nap. All of this his daughter did, and went off to work, leaving the house to his supervision. With babysitting there is a lot of time on one's hands. The old man on nice days would go out on the side deck and read to pass the time. It was during one of these off periods when the old man first noticed quite a lot of activity with the next door neighbors. The parents, a typical two income couple in their early forties, were at work, leaving their teenage son in the house alone. There was a lot of coming and going with teenagers driving up to the property. They would go into the house, and come out laughing and shouting, then drive away in their late model cars. As the weeks went by, the old man witnessed the same behavior. Many of these children came and left; almost like visiting a store. They weren't the same people each day, but the activities continued never-the-less.

"The kid was really popular," the old man thought, "or running some sort of business out of the house." Finally the old man mentioned the activities to his daughter. She wasn't sure what was going on, but did tell her father that the next door boy was rude and nasty to her and her children. When she spoke to his parents about it, they were defensive, and their attitude concerning her complaint, bordered on rudeness. She realized little would be accomplished in open dialogue with them, and didn't pursue it any further. She had little more to do about the situation, but to advise her kids to stay away from the aberrant teen. The old man's daughter appeared upset with the boy, but reluctant to follow-up any further with her father's concern.

The next door activities went on for several more weeks, and stimulated the old man's curiosity further. He was raised in the inner city, and knew about what he was seeing with his daughter's neighbor. It was almost typical: the drug dealer used children to distribute their drugs. They knew no adult would be home in the kid's house during the day, and who would be better able to sell drugs to other kids than a kid himself. In a discussion with his wife about this, the old man told her of his suspicion that the next door teen was selling drugs. "He never goes to school," the old man said to his wife. His wife was indifferent to her husband. "You don't know this," she retorted. "I'm from West Philadelphia," the old man reminded his spouse. "That stuff went on all the time there." Against his wife's opposition, the old man went to his daughter with his suspicions.

His daughter was even more disagreeable with her father's suspicions. "Tom and I can't go to the police with your suspicions. He'll get in trouble with the Bureau, if he approaches the police with all this. They will call his boss, he will give Tom a talking to about staying out of local police affairs. Is that what you want to do?"

"I don't want to get Tom in trouble," the old man replied; now becoming defensive, as if he was doing something wrong. "Shouldn't he at least know about all this, and keep an eye on what's going on? What is wrong with notifying the police; can't they work together with an FBI agent on something this serious?"

His daughter was now becoming agitated, and started to pace up and down. One of her older children entered the room, and began asking her questions about something unrelated to the conversation, she was having with her father. She used this as an excuse to end it. That night a call came through to the old man's house. It was his daughter; she didn't need him to baby sit any longer. She wouldn't speak to her father, nor return his phone calls nor visit his house for over two years after that night.

It was three years later when the old man's daughter called her mother. She was inviting her parents to a barbeque on the upcoming Sunday. They hadn't been there for some time. She rarely called her father directly. When she did, it was generally for something her husband couldn't do for her: a job around the house, or when she needed to talk to him about something, which was troubling her. The old man's wife was glad to receive the invitation; she missed the grandchildren.

"Well I'm going," she said to her husband, as if he wasn't. He said nothing in response; knowing her ways. Finally she came to him, and asked him directly, "You are going, aren't you?" "I am," he said.

It was after the meal, when the daughter came to her father. He knew something was wrong; she had that sad look in her eyes, the same look, as a little girl when troubled with something. The old man couldn't shut her up, when she had something on her mind, something, which was troubling her. His daughter wasn't crying, but he knew she was upset.

"He's dealing drugs next door," she blurted out, as if relieved to say it. She was referring to the same boy, her father spoke to her about three years earlier. Their driveway was adjacent with the daughter's property line, where the old man witnessed the drug dealing activities. The boy was no longer a boy; he was now a grown man, and still in business. The old man said nothing. He just listened to his second oldest daughter, allowing her to get it all off her chest. All her life she wanted a home like the one she had: beautiful, on the corner of a cul-de-sac, in a nice respectable community, with a good school district, and all one could find acceptable to raise children. Now she had what she and her husband worked so hard to get. There was a hitch; it came with a drug dealer living next door to her, operating freely in broad daylight. She didn't want to believe it, when her father revealed it to her, but she couldn't turn her back to it any longer. The truth has a way of coming to the surface, no matter how you try to stop it; it won't be denied. She went on with her story.

It was a warm sunny day, a school day. The school bus hadn't arrived yet, so her children weren't out on the cul-de-sac playing before dinner. An SUV, driven by a sixteen year old child with her friend in the shot-gun seat, sped around the bend of the main road. The driver, realizing she was about to miss the turn off to her destination, quickly turned the steering wheel into the development, where the old man's daughter and her family lived. The vehicle, unable to negotiate the maneuver, went over on its' side, landing on the daughter's driveway and lawn. Fortunately it didn't go over on its' top or the child driver and passenger would have been pinned inside. They were able to exit the vehicle with the help of a neighbor, who witnessed the accident. The two were visibly shaken with assorted cuts and bruises. The opinion of the neighbor and the old man's daughter, who also witnessed the affair, was the occupants were in need of going to the hospital for X-rays and a doctor's attention. However, when the police arrived and made this suggestion, they vehemently refused. Instead one of them called her parents on her cell phone, who immediately came and spirited both of them away.

The only information the youngsters gave the police was they were there to visit the boy next door, who wasn't available for questioning.

"He wasn't available, even though the girls came to visit him," the old man replied to fully construe his daughter's story.

"No he wasn't. Of course, the girls didn't want to go to the hospital, because they would discover, through blood tests and the like, the drugs in their systems. By law, the hospital has to report this to the police."

This time the son-in-law did go to the local police.

"Oh, we know all about him," the police detective replied to the FBI agent. The son-in-law was now questioning the township police on official Bureau business. That was all the daughter was able to say to her father. It might jeopardize the case against him, if it ever did go to court. To this date, the drug pusher was never arrested or ordered to go to court. He did move out of his parent's house for about six months, and came back continuing on with his business as usual. Don't ask me, why his parents put up with all this. Perhaps they aren't aware all this is going on in their own house. You know the three monkeys: see no evil, hear no evil, and speak no evil. Or perhaps, they are afraid of their son, and should be.

This is a true story, and on-going.

You may want to ask, "If the police know all about the drug pusher, then why isn't he in jail?" He isn't in jail, because the police can't get the evidence necessary to present the case to the District Attorney. They can't get the evidence, because they can't get a warrant to search his premises, and his victims (the users) aren't going to testify against him. This dirt bag continues in business, addicting young people with the poison he sells them. Keep in mind, besides addiction, these drugs have long lasting derogatory effects on their victims' thinking capacity and general health.

My partner and I detail drug addiction and its' effects in our book, "Everything You Should Know About the World's Environment, But Are Indifferent to Ask." Since we don't know what drugs the dirt bag is selling, the damage from them is only speculative.

All this goes on next door to an FBI agent in a nice neighborhood, which has a low crime rate. No wonder it's so low; the crimes seldom go to court, so they aren't considered crimes. The ones that do make it to court, well you know what the court does with them.

(18) In my lifetime the worse crime committed in the American Empire was 9/11; ranking up there with the Pearl Harbor attack by the Japanese, drawing the United States into the Second World War. 9/11 is the name given to the disastrous incidences of September 11, 2001 at the World Trade Center in New York City, and other disasters of that day. In chronological order the events went as follows.

8:45 A. M. American Airlines Flight 11, a Boeing 767 hijacked on route to Los Angeles, CA from Boston with 92 passengers aboard, slams into the north tower.

9:06 A. M. United Airlines Flight 175, also a Boeing 767 was hijacked routed from Boston to Los Angeles with 65 passengers aboard, banks hard and crashes through the south tower.

10:00 A. M. the south tower collapses trapping hundreds of rescuers below; this was in addition to perhaps thousands of workers in the structure. Debris guts the 4 World Trade Center building.

10:29 A. M. weakened by its imploding twin, the north tower also collapses, raining more debris, crushing buildings and rescuers below.

5:25 P. M. fires and debris take their toll, and the 7 World Trade Center falls.

Although the crashes were devastating, the belief was the fires caused by it should have been isolated to the top floors only, and the rest of the buildings would be held intact. That information was incorrect; both buildings collapsed in their entirety. Here is the reason given for this happening. Each tower (approximately 200 feet wide) contained a central steel core, surrounded by open office space. Eighteen inch steel tubes ran vertically along the outside, giving most of the support for the building. When the plane damaged the central core, the weight was redistributed to the outer steel tubes, which in turn were gradually deformed by the added weight and the heat of the fires. The result was each building was left without support, which started a chain reaction of each floor crashing down on the other, until the buildings were a total pile of rubble, killing thousands of people inside.

(18)Source: Port Authority of New York and New Jersey, and TIME Magazine

There were other attacks that day: American Flight 77, Washington, DC to Los Angeles, CA with 64 people aboard crashed into the Pentagon, 9:40 A.M.; a passenger on United Flight 93, Newark, NJ to San Francisco, CA with 45 passengers aboard, called the emergency operator in Pennsylvania revealing their plane was being hijacked.   At 10:00 A.M. the jet crashed 80 miles southeast of Pittsburgh, PA.   Apparently the passengers aboard overpowered the terrorists, and avoided an attack on a site in Washington, DC, which was believed to be the White House.

My partner and I for the scope of this paper have decided to concentrate more on the New York City disasters for now.   Before doing so, it is important that we acknowledge the heroism of the Flight 93 passengers.   Bravery is still with us as a nation, and has given us hope coming out of a day of multiple disasters.   Secondly, we ask for God's grace for all the victims and their loved ones of that day's massacre (3,035 innocent people dead, total).   Have mercy on their souls, dear God.

They deserve better in the next life, than what they got here on earth.

On the surface nineteen dead hijackers were responsible for 9/11. There is more to the story than this group of criminals and their ambitions. Since Cain and Abel, there have been criminals and murderers; they have been a part of this earth, since the beginning, and unfortunately will be with us until the end. It is easy to say the 9/11 criminals did it all, and they are the sole perpetrators of this terrible crime. The fact is the crime didn't end with the doers of it. There were two others, who made it possible: one, the leadership of the American Empire, and two, the builders of the twin towers, were equally responsible. When a country, such as the United States, is soft in dealing with crime, it leaves itself open to terrorist assaults of the 9/11 nature, since it protects the wrongdoers, and allows them to go about their business without challenge. They have their rights, and the victim isn't taken into consideration in the Empire's pursuit of this terrible miscarriage of justice. So, when the FBI agent presented President G. Walker Bush with the possibility of 9/11 taking place, he didn't act on the warning.   Although it is true that his lack of action on the advice was poor, it does agree with the American mindset of being soft on crime.   Every day in the lives of the American Empire, crimes similar to those which happened on 9/11 take place.   They are allowed by the police, who know that the arrested felons have little chance of being prosecuted in the American court system.   In breaking down the crimes; they are stealing, destruction of private property and murder. Granted they are of a lesser nature than 911, but never–the–less they are crimes with victims, who are ignored under the system.   The mindset protecting these criminals also protected the nineteen hijackers on 9/11.

Consequently 3000 plus victims are dead, and billions of dollars are lost in the American and worldwide economies, as a result of this multiple tragedy.   The victims' loved ones aren't vindicated for their losses, and the most powerful city in the American Empire has been seriously crippled economically and spiritually.

Years ago, when I was a boy my mother told me the fable of the Three Pigs.   Briefly there were three pigs, who were just starting out, and needed to build homes for themselves to protect them from the big bad wolf. The first pig decided to build a house, made out of straw. This was a total failure; when the wolf came around, he blew the structure down, and ate the pig. The second pig constructed a house made out of twigs; the same fate happened to him as the first pig. The third pig, seeing the fate of the other pigs, was smarter and more resourceful. He built his house out of bricks and mortar. When the wolf visited him, no matter how much he huffed and puffed, he couldn't knock down the brick house, and the third pig survived.

Shortly after the 9/11 disaster, one of the network television stations interviewed the head architect, who designed the twin towers. His testimony, or at least that is how it sounded, described the building's structure in detail, explaining how the two structures collapsed under the impact of the planes' on the towers. I've given you that information earlier. It immediately reminded me of the Three Pig's fable. I can only hope the builders and designers of the new World Trade Center buildings (four of them under construction) will abide by the lesson taught by the wisdom of this story, and keep in mind there is always a wolf out there somewhere, who will eat you, if you show him a weakness.

The head architect was in near tears, when he gave the American public on network television his rendition of the buildings' structural design, and so he should be. Each floor in the buildings should have been self-contained in the event of a fire or explosion; they weren't. A better grade of steel should have been used in the main supports. The proof of this is how readily the steel tubes (main support) melted from the fire's heat; it shouldn't have. How in the name of God did this lackluster design ever pass the building codes? Who is held accountable for all this?

The two stories tell you what crime is in the American Empire, and what to expect from the Justice System in your country. It is good to be clear on what you're up against. By acknowledging this you can go to the next level, and find out why all this is happening to you. When you know what the disease is, you can find a cure for it. For our part, my partner and I will keep digging, until we find answers. We will write about them, and confirm our suspicions with proof and suggestions on what you the public can do about the problem. We remain confident that there is a plot in the Empire, set in motion by the powers (the money interests), who run it. What that plot is, we don't know. The Supreme Court has endorsed this notion in Miranda v. Arizona 1966 (due process clause of the 14th Amendment of the Constitution). The mandate began a nightmare of lawlessness against the American public in the form of arrested and convicted criminals being set free, because of some technicality determined by the courts. Their verdicts have put the law abiding citizens under the gun. Their safety and the safety of their children is compromised. The criminals rule for now. With all the hopelessness which appears to overshadow you, the public, you can take heart, since you are still the ultimate power. Just as the truth will eventually win out, so you the people will win. My partner and I are dedicated to this victory. The answers are out there. We don't know what they are for now, but we will.

"The ones who calls the shots, won't be among the dead and lame."

A line from an old song: Christmas in the

Trenches, WW–I

End of CRIME

THE SAD SIXTIES

Old people are looked down on in the American Empire. They are early retired in most industries, being forced out of the system, and generally disrespected by a country they were most generous to by contributing in the form of taxes, military duty, obeying its' law, and running its' commerce. Much of this was documented earlier, so we won't go into the statistics of this discrimination. Instead we want to evaluate the "why" aspect of this assault on the country's seniors.

The one advantage older Americans have over their juniors, is they lived in a time when life in our country was better, so the powers want to discredit us and shut out the knowledge we possess concerning that period. I believe they've done this quite successfully. In preparing this essay my partner, a considerably younger man, has given way to me in assembling much of the data, and intervenes only with his skilled legal mind in keeping the comments from going over the edge, which would invite a possible law suit. However, our suspicions are the same concerning the emergence of the American Empire and its' misconception of justice. We date this as coming out of the sixties, beginning with the death of President John F. Kennedy in 1963. This was solidified with the Woodstock Music Festival of August, 1969, which had a lasting effect on the youth of the United States, since its fame went beyond the borders of that small town, becoming nationwide and then worldwide. These young people grew up, and became our leaders and policy makers. The damage done at Woodstock (mainly sex outside of marriage and illegal drug taking) to the values once possessed, has turned our nation into a country void of moral values. I'm not being a prude here. Think about it. The main products sold by the criminal elements in America are black market drugs, and prostitution. Both are multibillion dollar industries. To put crime out of business you take away the demand for these two products. They exist because the American people want them to exist. Also keep in mind giving money to criminals is giving them power to operate and grow. It also gives them guns to murder and kill innocent people, and fancy lawyers to defend them in a court of law.

These and other values lost will be revealed in comparing the fifties and the sixties. It is our contention all of this wasn't a coincidence: a pattern was to develop from the sixties' period; although not a plan per se, but a direction along the wrong path.

My adolescent years were spent in the nineteen fifties, which were known to the youth of the sixties, as the sad fifties. The decade was given this name, because the sixties youth considered themselves more hip about what was going on in the country and the world, and were more involved in protesting and the like, than the obedient fifties youth. I first wrote this paper back in the mid-seventies, rewrote it in 2002 and now in 2009. What I found out with each rewrite was, there was more information available to me during each period, since history was providing it. History has a way of drawing forth the truth, because it isn't affected by fads or news reporting gimmicks. All it says is this is what happened, when it happened, and why, and most important this is the result of the event in the long run. You already know the result; what we are going to show you is what you lost, before it happened.

The fifties was a beautiful time for me, even though I had the least in my life financially. It's curious how most people associate happiness with money. I can take a cruise, buy new clothes, get out of this place, buy a new car, and get my old lady's breasts enlarged. People go on dreaming about hitting the lottery, or when their ship will come in, and it all takes place with money. For me, happiness was in the fifties. I had friends, good health, played sports every day, chased after girls at night, went down the shore in the summer, whenever I had a few extra bucks to take the bus. In the winter, when it snowed I went sledding in the park, and had snow ball fights. School was good, even though occasionally boring, but I still learned. I was young, and my life was ahead of me, waiting for me to catch up to it. My manhood was emerging like a rush; no longer was I a kid; I was now a gawky, skinny six foot man child, ready to conquer the world. I felt free even though there was little to be free about. I was still under the control of my parents, who were poor like everybody else in the neighborhood. We didn't care; when you never had money, you never seem to miss it. We just went from one day to the next doing whatever we had to do to get by. Few neighbors had cars, so you didn't worry about car payments, and who had the latest model. Not many homes had television, so we went out to entertain ourselves; the youngsters played sports and outside games; the older people visited other neighbors and talked and listened. If you needed anything like food staples or medicine, a food market or drug store was within walking distance. Anything further than that, you could reach by public transportation. The average person walked a lot, and was outside most of the time; especially in the summer, since air conditioning was rare. With a fewer number of cars on the road; car accidents were less common, and air pollution wasn't the threat it is today. A teenager was lucky, if he could get a part time job after school, so he turned his attention to sports or work around the house to fix it up or whatever chores his parents asked him to do. You did what you were told. You could buy an old car for about twenty five bucks, and PEP Boys was always somewhere close by in the neighborhood to help a teen get it running. Young women had to work around the house helping mom, and do babysitting jobs to make a few bucks. They played some sports, did cheerleading or were in the high school band or school plays.

Back then I didn't even know what college was, let alone attend one. I was set to be a laborer just as my father and father's father were, so there was no pressure to keep my marks up in school. After the Korean War was over, we enjoyed ten years of peace. Although the draft hung over our heads after high school, most of us gave little thought to it. Some of us looked on it as a chance to travel before settling down into raising a family of our own. From a teen's perspective, there was little pressure put on us. We had a chance to be kids, and enjoy life a little, until having to give way to the pressures of being adults. So without early stress to succeed in the work force, nor worry about going into combat or keeping up with the Jones', all we had to do was grow up, which by itself is pretty challenging. One other point of significance, suicide among adolescents back then, was much lower.

Additionally in the fifties period, we had

relatively few instances of scandal, either locally or nationally in our government, or with business and religious leaders. Consequently, there was greater respect in the minds of our youth for the system, and who ran it.

The term, "generation gap," was unknown back in the fifties. Your parents ran the household, and you conformed to their wishes, and rules of the home. With all this regulatory behavior, no teen felt pressured, nor put upon. Instead, we knew what was expected of us. With it all, we were still close to mom and dad, because our parents weren't afraid to show love and affection. They were interested in us, but not possessive. They advised, but didn't control. They disciplined, but did not harm. Few of them knew nor practiced any fancy child psychology. If a young person was wrong, he was corrected for it, and went on from there. Seldom did a teen go home to an empty house. Mom was there for advice and consultation with a problem, and a hot home cooked meal. There is something to be said about getting it off your chest, and no better way of doing it than over a full plate of food. Most teens today can't do this. Mom and dad have their own careers; the adolescent has to make an appointment with them to be heard, and by then it is often too late. Illegal drug use wasn't a problem of the magnitude it is today. We knew about these substances, but never used them, because they were socially unacceptable. In its' place we drank beer on occasions. The exciting thing to do was to see what bars in the neighborhood would serve us. There were always a few in the general area, where the criterion for getting a brew was based on whether you were tall enough to put your money up on the bar. So we weren't perfect, but who is?

Every Friday night my buddies, and I would go over to the Hill bar, and my one friend who looked the oldest, would go in and get us a few quarts of beer to get us oiled up for the local church dance. Regardless of the weather, we would drink it in a nearby park, and talk about how cool we were, and what chicks we knew, that we would like to get to know better. From there we walked over to the parish dance to meet some of the chicks, we were just dreaming about; hopeful to take one of them home afterwards, and perhaps steal a good night kiss at her doorstep. Smelling like the cheap beer we just drank, and weaving a little, we would dance our way into the dance. The Stroll dance was popular back then, so we waited for this type of music to begin and for the Stroll line to take shape. Without removing our overcoats, we picked out one of the chicks in the line, and danced into the auditorium, where the dance was held. This and our apparent inebriated condition made us look cool and grown up with the girls, and they took delight in our daring to go to a church dance bombed out of our heads, even though we weren't. You do whatever you can to impress the opposite sex. At least that's how we felt about it back then.

It was less complex making friends back in the fifties; regardless of age. People were more outgoing and approachable. We were this way, since most people stayed in the general community for generations; speaking to each other casually was natural and unencumbered. The new face of a neighbor was welcomed, and soon fit in, as if they were a long term member. Folks were considerate of the next guy. Unnecessary outside noise, like basketball playing in the driveway and loud radios were unheard of by the residents.

Parties and other celebrations were held indoors. Neighbors were up front with each other, and could offer a complaint without expecting a reprisal and bad feelings about it. Try doing that today.

Approaching the opposite sex, like making friends in general, was less compromising. A young woman wasn't afraid to strike up a conversation with a young man, since she wasn't concerned with him being a pervert or a person of questionable character. Those people were in jail. The dating process was more formal; you had to tell the girl's parents where you were going and have her home by a certain hour. The places for interacting with the opposite sex were more available. We had the church dances, drug store soda fountains, hoagie shops, and Juke Box joints where we could get a burger and fries and listen to the latest music. The difference was the streets were safer; you could go anywhere you wanted without concern about getting mugged or attacked. In short we had our civil liberties. This would begin to erode in the late sixties, coinciding with the eroding of moral values in general.

Young girls in the fifties weren't sexually permissive, and young men respected a nice young lady. A party could be held in one's home without concern for how the young guests would behave themselves. All social interactions were local, within the community. The sixties would change all this as more and more teens out of high school attended the different colleges. This created a more widespread socialization opportunity, since the students were from all parts of the country, leaving their neighborhoods, and relocating to the university campus. The school itself became a new atmosphere for social behavior among the young. The changes in moral behavior were monumental, since parental guidance ended sooner for the sixties child, and the colleges were reluctant or indifferent in replacing it. The fraternities and sororities with all their bad living conditions and lack of supervision replaced parents and home values for many young Americans beginning in the sixties. Since most of the country's national leaders were college trained, it stands to reason their values were likewise influenced by this campus environment. What evolved was a drastic shift from traditional values and morality, which affected American living. Now we all have the following: illegal drug taking, sex outside of marriage, disrespect for family living, acceptance of homosexuality, a falling away from religious beliefs and morality, and less respect for one's neighbor. All this leaves many in our country with depression and anger, and they don't know, why. There aren't enough pills and booze, one can take, to make it go away.

In the fifties we had Senator Joseph R. McCarthy and his highly publicized hearings, where he accused army officials, members of the media, and other public figures of being Communist. This stimulated further the Cold War with the Soviet Union and the possibility of nuclear confrontation, which became a national concern, bordering on paranoia. Acting quickly the Senate did their own investigation of their colleague from Wisconsin, and concurred his accusations were false and exposed him on national television. This brought the country back to a semblance of well-being concerning the Communist threat. If you have dirty laundry, then clean it; don't leave it around stinking up the place. The US Congress did just that.

In the sixties, the leaders didn't take this advice, and left their dirty laundry laying around throughout the decade. It smelled so bad, that it split the country in half; robbing the American people of their trust in the government. The era began with the assassination of one of our greatest and most popular presidents, John F. Kennedy. The circumstances of the murder were distorted, when our leadership attempted to cover up many of the facts surrounding the assassination with the Warren Report. The document was hastily put together by high ranking officials in the government, summarizing what took place, and who was guilty of the killing. It ended all further investigation into the crime by the local Dallas police or the Federal Bureau of Investigation. Again getting back to history, it was later proven and documented in this writing that the report was filled with lies and half–truths, and deliberately distorted any facts it did uncover. Our reason for reviewing it again is to remind the reader of the sixties disaster and the beginning factor in the destruction of the American lifestyle and how it would be a major contributor in driving the country from a republic to the American Empire. Showing power is power, and it can even get away with murdering the President of the United States, if it so chooses.

Viet Nam, a small nation in Southeast Asia, was undergoing a civil war between the north and south during the sixties. Fearing this conflict would aid the spread of communism in the region, President Kennedy sent military advisors to the south of this country. It is mentioned here not to rehash what was covered earlier in the book, but to remind the reader this action would go against popular opinion, and drive a further wedge between our government and the will of the people. The war lasted eight years; cost billions of dollars, which greatly harmed the economy, and most importantly resulted in the death of over 37,000 American fighting men. Our involvement in Viet Nam's war was considered a holding action, so we weren't there to win or lose. From where I stand, our country paid more for this holding action than what was obvious and up front. Our greatest price paid was the disruption of the faith the American citizen had in its' leadership. From the death of President Kennedy and the Viet Nam War escalation, the distrust would grow to other institutions as well: religion and morality, schooling, educational principles, and how the average American would interact in his community with his neighbors. It took root in the sixties and is still with us, causing untold damage to every phase of American living. Hurting the American where he lives, so to speak; this is the greatest loss of all.

Hair styles for young men in the fifties were the wet look with a pompadour, in which the hair was combed back and up with perhaps some hair coming out of place, centered on the forehead. In the back, the hair was trained to resemble a duck's behind or DA (Duck's Ass), since it resembled this, if you had the imagination to see it. The actor Tony Curtis and rock singer Elvis Presley had the perfect styling for the period. A cool teen always had a comb in his back pocket, and would occasionally run it through his hair as needed to keep the DA as perfect as possible. The teenage girls mostly kept their hair pulled back in a ponytail, when they were active, copying the actress Sandra Dee. On special occasions they wore their hair shoulder length, imitating the actress Veronica Lake, with a part of the hair covering one eye. On very, very special occasions they wore it in back in a French twist, like the actress Kim Novak.

All styles in the period were geared towards the cool look. The kids didn't want to be like their parents in style, but they didn't want to look like slobs either. Guys wore pegged pants, where the trousers were baggy in the upper part of the legs and tight in the ankle areas. With this the pants had saddle stitching down the legs and high rise belt loops, the loops beginning about two inches from the top. Teen girls dressed in the full poodle skirts with plenty of petticoats underneath to make it puff out. They also wore tighter fitting skirts, which went well below the knees. With both skirts, they often wore tight fitting pastel sweaters, with padded bras. I never forgot the tight sweaters. Both sexes wore dungarees and loafers with white sweat socks. Dungarees never go out of style, or so it seems.

In contrast the sixties' look was casual and unkempt. The young men didn't shave or cut their hair; wore sun faded jeans, tie-dyed shirts and sandals. They were too busy pursuing intellectual matters and protesting to be bothered bathing. Girls followed pretty much the same mold. The idea was the unisex look, which represented the belief in sexual equality. Dresses were for squares, who conformed to the system. Girls were burning their bras in protest rallies, but women's underwear sales continued to rise. Just goes to show you, when a female needs to divide and separate and lift, the bra is the best way to do it. The need is what the market looks for, and so it responded accordingly. If the decade was producing a generation of disorganized slobs, who couldn't clean up after themselves, the market would answer the call. They did this with house cleaning services, lawn care landscapers, interior decorators, house painters, etc., who would do the work previously done by the homeowners a generation ago.

(19) I don't want to leave the sixties casual dress code just yet. It is important, because it would have a lasting effect on how future generations would dress, going into the twenty first century. Two famous Rock entertainers coming out of the sixties, stand out in my mind with the casual look: Jimi Hendrix and Janis Joplin. Why marginal talents like these two have so much influence on people is beyond me, but they do, and as such, should be evaluated to see why. I'll do it briefly.

Hendrix, a psychedelically inspired guitarist, told LIFE Magazine in an interview (1969) the following: "Musicians hypnotize people, and can preach into the subconscious what we want to say." Maybe Jimi was right; perhaps he and Janis did just that. Look around. Many Americans dress and look like them: tired, shabbily dressed, hair all over the place, in a hurry, no values, probably on some sort of drugs. A year later both entertainers would be dead; Joplin from a heroin overdose; Hendrix from a drug-related asphyxiation.

(19)LIFE Sixty Years, by the Editors of Life, A 60th Anniversary   Celebration 1936 – 1996

Rock 'n Roll was invented in the fifties. I first heard it on a black radio station. Black stars such as Ben E. King, Patti LaBelle, Tina Turner and others would emerge on the scene. Not a bad list, but Rock 'n Roll wasn't limited to black stars alone. A small record company in Nashville, TN would produce super stars: Elvis Presley, Roy Orbison and Johnny Cash. Philadelphia PA had American Bandstand with Dick Clark; a televised program to give talented entertainers exposure, which eventually went nationwide. Detroit MI had Motown Record Company, California had The Beach Boys, and New Orleans LA had Fats Domino, and of course Chuck Berry was from everywhere. I could go on for many more pages. The artists were all colors, creeds and backgrounds. There were no crossover artists then, only American music people who played good Rock 'n Roll. They influenced one another, and the music developed and improved. It came from the streets, bars, dances, churches, anywhere a talented person could get up and do his thing. It belonged to no one, but was owned by everybody. It was America's music. I never heard anything like it; you could dance and sing to it, like nothing I ever knew. The songs came from the heart, from everyday folks. The talent base was enormous. The hits kept coming, as if they would never end.

In the sixties the music changed. It no longer was America's music; it became the world's music. The Beatles, the Rolling Stones, the Bee Gees, and Elton John would have a serious impact on it, altering it to a certain refinement, which was more acceptable as a standard music form. Not to say that America didn't stay competitive. They did with artists such as Simon and Garfunkel, Bob Dylan, Smokey Robinson, Michael Jackson, and of course (the King) Elvis Presley. The above are artists, who immediately come to mind; don't be offended, if we left out anyone of your favorites. The omission wasn't intentional.

From the sixties music went big time and eventually would be controlled by mega large corporations. It would fully reach this point somewhere in the nineteen eighties, and when it did, the music died, and the people were given what the large companies wanted to give them. If you don't believe me, ask yourself, who are the big stars of today in the music business, do they have any talent, and will they be remembered? Do you remember them? Do you go around humming one of their songs, during the course of your day?

Illegal drugs became the cool thing to do in the sixties. I'm not sure why. Americans are people, who give way to fads. When something gets going, and the right people (Hendrix and Joplin?) start doing it, then it snowballs, and pretty soon everybody is doing it. In our opinion drug addiction was the saddest consequence of the Sad Sixties. We go over the hazards of their use in our book, "Everything You Should Know About The World's Environment, But Are Indifferent To Ask!" We aren't going to reinvent the wheel by detailing them in this work, but the effects are so important that a review should be briefly mentioned.

1. Drug overdoses – Since a doctor isn't controlling the doses; overdoses are prevalent, as Jimi and Janis found out.

2. Permanent brain damage to the users over a period of time.

3. The purchases give enormous sums of money to organized crime, strengthening their operations.

4. Drugs are responsible for industrial accidents i.e. 1989 Prince William Sound, Alaska. Exxon Valdez hit an undersea reef and released 100 million gallons of oil into the waters. The ship's Captain was under the influence of illegal drugs.

5. Illegal drug users (and drunk drivers) are responsible for a large percentage of highway collisions e. g. recently in the Philadelphia area a drunk driver hit and killed two motorists, who were resolving a minor fender bender accident on an off ramp. The driver of the SUV, who hit them, was

speeding and under the influence of illegal drugs.

6. Money spent on illegal drugs isn't money well spent. It could be better used on legal buying, and also taxed relieving the tax burden.

7. A drug addicted mother can have a baby born with a deformity, and with the very addiction the mother has. Hospital nurses and doctors look for the latter with these mothers, and will hold the baby over to treat the addiction.

To sum all this up, the sixties, to an older person, represented sad times; not the fifties. The fifties with all their regulations were the happy times. I believe many sixties teens, who are grown adults now, know this to be true. What made it especially sad was the sixties children won every battle in their demonstrations and revolutionary thinking, but lost the war, since they brought our country into a worse condition, than it was before. Their victories turned into disasters. Here is what we inherited from them.

..Casual sex before marriage became an introduction to a new incurable AIDS virus, which is spread through sexual promiscuity.

..Legalized abortion, with a death count in

the millions of unborn babies. This has given way to protests and a split in the country concerning the morality of the procedures.

..Recreational illegal drug taking has led to serious drug addiction problems, as previously listed. In the sixties the drugs were supposed to enhance creativity, but in fact did the opposite, leaving the victim a slave to the instant habit, which comes out of using the substances.

..Homosexuality is now considered an alternate life style, instead of being a form of mental illness and immorality.

The peace demonstrations of the sixties did very little to bring peace to the country, since the children of the period, with all their freedom issues gave no credence to the freedom of their fellow Americans, who were forced to listen to their loud music and disruptive practices. In time this non-concern for the feelings of others, melted into the culture as acceptable behavior. A side practice coming out of the period was a rudeness most Americans have for one another. "The finger," has become a symbol of this insulting reaction, especially when people are driving an automobile.

It is so well known, that I only need to mention it, without any explanation for the reader to understand what it means.

Morality has been replaced by getting away with whatever you can. The generation gap of the sixties was the forerunner of this, because the children of the period went against parental authority in the home. Up until then, the parents were the main teachers of right and wrong principles. When these values began eroding in the sixties: integrity, fair play, good manners, the golden rule, etc. all suffered, since they are the outgrowth of morality.

Americans aren't allowed to pray in the public schools, where a good chunk of our local tax money goes. Why, because a rich atheist said so, and was backed up by a Supreme Court ruling. It produced little national outcry, because the Darwinian evolutionary principles of the sixties prevailed in American thinking. The ruling stretches separation of church and state to the point of illogical outrage, and curtails freedom of religion, the other part of the first amendment in the Bill of Rights. One must question, as we do, what other topics our children will be told they aren't allowed to speak about or discuss in our schools?   All this came out of the freedom bigots, who protested in the sad sixties.

In closing I realize I've been quite negative about the sixties.   Surely something good came out of the period, but I can't think what it was.   My main attempt, and not to excuse it, was to compare it to the fifties, and to challenge the youth of the sixties calling the fifties a sad time.   It was anything else but.   With few exceptions, I look back on the fifties with fondness, and a character building time for me.   For the sixties, I believe it was a time for the youth of the period to escape; not to benefit by.

End of: THE SAD SIXTIES

SUPPLY AND DEMAND

(20) This chapter will be devoted to how the American Empire works. Two powers drive the Empire: one is called the Republican Party (the party of the rich and big business), and the other is called the Democratic Party (the people's party or coalition party). The Republicans represent supply; the Democrats represent demand. No matter what the politicians tell you and promise you, you will know who they are, and what they represent by this means of identification. Make no mistake about it; it is what it is, and will always be this way until the Empire comes to an end. The first thing we were taught at Wharton Business School as freshmen, was the principle of "Caveat Emptor" (Latin phrase for, let the buyer beware). Briefly it means in a buying/selling relationship, it is the responsibility of the buyer to satisfy himself concerning the quality of the goods or services he receives. This phrase is the very backbone of the Republican Party, when it is in power, at any level (local, state or federal). The Democrats take the opposite stand; they insist it is

the responsibility of the seller concerning the quality of the goods and services sold. Next to the Marine Corps motto, "Semper Fidelis" (or Always Faithful), "Caveat Emptor" is the most important Latin, I was ever taught. My partner and I ask that you keep the latter foremost in your mind, as we take you through the principles of Supply and Demand. Yes, the two are tied in with politics and power.

I can still remember the words of my college economics professor, whenever a question concerning some current event pertaining to the economy was raised in class discussion. He would begin by using the traditional supply and demand curve chart to approach and identify the related problems involved, and how the powers in charge should go about solving them.

"In its' simplest form," my teacher would enumerate. "We have a market for a valued commodity or service." He would draw a right angle to represent this on the blackboard. One side of the angle was demand; the other showed supply. He would then add curves, which indicated how the two interacted with one another at the equilibrium point, or where demand perfectly met supply in the market place.

"This very simple design is at the heart of free world economic principles," he went on to say. "Briefly, it illustrates as supply increases, demand is lessoned and vice-versa. In order not to oversimplify anything about the phenomena, a strategist can apply this principle to any problem affecting whatever is being sold in the market place. From here, a plan can be formulated to identify a problem in it, and to make adjustments accordingly. The trick is, there are various ideas about how to go about doing this adjustment."

I wrote this paper back in 1974, when our country was going through the worse inflation, I can ever remember. In evaluating it, the problem was brought on by an increase in demand (broadened markets) or a decrease in supply (caused by a lessening of production or a lack of raw materials, or both). For my own edification, I continued on from there, and wrote it all down to see if any of it was understandable, and applicable to the principles explained to me at the university.

To begin. The question we must ask is what side of the economy is causing the difficulty? Careful consideration must be given in formulating the answer to the possibility that both sides (supply or demand) may be the cause; perhaps one more than the other.

"Is it from the demand side?" I questioned myself, and went on from there. This is the user side, which basically comes down to people and their needs. People are users and consumers, and as such make up demand. To properly understand demand, we must understand what makes people tick for they are the markets, where demand is born and nurtured. What customers want, and have the ability to pay for, constitutes demand. This is very important in evaluating this side of the economy. If desire and ability to buy are affected in any way, it could greatly influence the behavior of the system, which affects us all. With this in mind, we can examine demand as a cause of inflation.

First off, demand in general has increased over the years, not only in the United States, but in foreign markets as well. This has been brought about by a steady population growth and the opening of foreign trade. The question here is, is demand increasing faster than suppliers are willing or able to keep up with? I use the words, "are willing," here, because producers may not want to maximize output, since this may not optimize profits. I'll discuss this further, as I get into the supply side of the equation, since this by itself could spur on inflation.

Concentrating more on demand, demand is growing, as I stated, due to the rise in population and new markets. However, an interesting turn of events is taking place with regard to demand for certain commodities. For example, the sale of new automobiles has dropped this year (1974) as compared to the previous year's sales. (Note: The same can be said for the year 2009, since similar events occurred to prompt the decline). To understand it better one has to look at the average consumers' hierarchy of needs. Number one, food is purchased before any other commodity, so it is obvious to rank it before any other need, since we all have to eat in order to survive. Number two, would be medical care, especially with older people. Number three, is housing, and housing related products and services such as home heating, electricity, etc. Four, is the automobile and automobile dependent products: gasoline, tires, batteries, etc. Five, is clothing, which is similar to cars, since the consumer can always use last year's styles. Six, is entertainment; this encompasses vacations, eating out, going to shows and movies, buying a new television, attending sporting events, etc. The hierarchy list goes on, and can be interpreted differently by different analysts, but it always comes out the same: according to how much the consumer has at his disposal to spend, and how he decides to use his limited income. If one industry draws too much from this income, then the others will suffer according to the hierarchy. For example, if food products rise exorbitantly then it could affect the buying power for needs two, three, four, etc. on down the line. Simply put, if you don't have money for a commodity or service, you can't buy it.

Now I'm assuming the consumer is prudent and properly budgets his income, which isn't always the case, since he is sometimes affected by a thing called fads. A case in point is the craze for the Sport Utility Vans or SUVs, which began in nineteen nineties, and is still with us today. These vehicles cost more to buy and operate, but consumers love them, and are willing to go the extra expense in order to satisfy their desires. I've already gone over the whys and wherefores of this demand in an earlier chapter, so I won't repeat myself. The point here is, this fad is taking away buying power from other industries, and in so doing is affecting the economy.

Now there is another influence on the hierarchy of demand and disposable income, it is called buying on credit, or buy now and pay later. This is an avenue of fad buying, and can throw off the hierarchy of needs, but not for long, since like money it will run out because this is regulated by a control called a personal credit rating. When it reaches a certain low point, the piper must be paid. Here, the hierarchy of needs kicks in and the idiot consumer, who abuses his credit will eventually have to comply with the reality of overspending.

Getting back to my point of disposable income, the consumer will react to wherever it takes him. If he can't afford a new car, he will put it off, and make do with last year's model. This occurring throughout the market place will cause the sales of new cars to drop. Since the automobile industry and related industries are so

vital to the nation's economy, another element will
occur: unemployment, which also affects demand.
If you don't make money, you can't spend what
you don't have, and that also goes for credit
buying. And the beat goes on. Here we not only
have buying power affecting demand, but
production as well. This has a devastating
influence on many industries, causing their sales to
drop off sharply. Other industries, which provide
needs higher up on the hierarchy list, generally
aren't affected as much immediately, and may be
tempted to raise their prices. Profits resulting from
this aren't due to innovative techniques coming out
of the industry, but are the result of price raising on
an industry wide scale, much like a monopoly
interaction. This is counterproductive, since it
harms the very economy the industry is operating
in, and is inflationary by nature. To go against this
rule, although tempting, is foolish, and self–
destructive. This must be avoided, no matter what
is going on in the market.

Let's say the country goes into an
inflationary period. If the consumer is paying more
for his needs, because of this problem, can it be
that inflation will correct itself, when demand goes

down i.e. the natural reaction of the market place?
I would doubt it.   The best that can be said is,
lessened demand will slow inflation down.
However, other factors must come into play such
as, government intervention, and human nature or
a desire by the people in the market place to
control rising prices.   Of course, with all problem
solving notions one must factor in, "all things being
equal."   The latter is an unexpected happening,
which occurs when you don't expect it, i.e. acts of
God such as weather related mishaps.   You'll
know it, when it happens. Consequently, with all
this in mind, then demand becomes an instrument
in fighting inflation.   This is only part of the
picture.

As I intimated earlier, there is another
situation, which occurs when the economy is in
trouble, such as it is with inflation.   People lose
their jobs.   This causes a recessionary period, or a
slowdown in the economy: sales are off,
production drops, and job layoffs follow.   No jobs
mean less money to purchase, and so forth; one
situation leads to another, and the country goes
into economic decline.   So it is that demand is
affected, not because it isn't there.   It is, but

without money, the consumer can't do anything about his demand. When this happens, prices should go down or at least stabilize, but this does not always take place. Under a purist economy, where there is perfect competition, prices should go down or stabilize, but the real world isn't pure or perfect. To comprehend why prices don't necessarily stabilize, we must look at the supply side of the problem.

Supply in certain industries can be controlled by the organizations, which make available the supply. When this takes place, the economy is no longer free. Consequently, to solve a problem in such a business environment, different strategies must be employed. First off, attention should be given to this supply control: if it exits, to what extent, and controlled by whom. Today most industries in the supply side live in big business, or should I say huge business. Since our nation is a car driven economy (no pun intended), it doesn't take much to figure out this is the best place to begin in understanding the supply side. For me, I like to study one step behind the car, which brings us to the energy which fuels it, oil. This is the key industry in the United States.

What happens here affects all the other industries.

Back in 1973, the oil industry came under control; not by an American monopoly, but by an international cartel called OPEC or the Oil Producing Energy Countries. This monopoly was created because the United States and other western countries became dependent on other nations for their oil needs. These energy supplying countries got together and organized a cartel, which set production quantities and prices for their oil. This took America by surprise, since it was a key industry, and the result of this cartel creation set off an inflationary trend unprecedented in the nation's history. It all began during one of the many Arab/Israel Wars, when the Arab States decided, as a retaliatory measure (mostly against the USA) to place an embargo on all oil shipments to nations supplying arms and other aid to the small Israeli state. Up until then, little thought was given to how much the United States depended on foreign oil. There were estimates ranging from five to twenty percent of the overall need. It turned out to be more than most people thought; much more. From here, it was just a matter of time before all the oil producing countries figured it out, and got together to do what American industries were doing for years: fixing production rates and prices. It began with a second embargo to show that the new cartel was united. They indeed were, and from that time on oil production would never be the same, since the supply and cost of this critical commodity would seriously be influenced by OPEC controls.

Note: There were some critics of the large oil oligopolies in America, who alleged that the American oligopolies got into bed, so to speak, with OPEC to share the wealth and further control prices from their side of the supply. My partner and I wouldn't put it past them to do so. We will develop this further, but there is more to discuss about supply, which will better lead into this possibility.

Getting back to the OPEC formation, and its' impact on America and their reaction to it. The country did nothing to combat it at the time. They simply capitulated, and in time the nation was thrown into galloping inflation. The American voter responded by electing out of office the present administration. Sadly, the next president didn't do any more than his predecessor, and the country continued on with its' inflation, until it suddenly came to an end. Why? My partner and I can't answer that question for now. We are working on it. Two interesting developments came out of this dilemma: one, a larger percentage of Americans began driving more gas efficient smaller cars, and two, the oil companies with their increased revenues were given incentives to explore for new sources of oil, which would increase supply.

Let me note, the automobile manufacturers didn't come up with research concerning alternate fuel for cars. Since there were no competing energy products, nor the threat of one coming along in the immediate future, the oil industry had carte blanche, and could charge any price they wanted. Keep in mind all this took place in the nineteen seventies. In the twenty first century, automakers did invent alternatively fueled cars (part battery/gasoline driven autos). This is hardly an alternative, but a step in the right direction. The manufacturers' problem here is the oil companies refused to carry other fuel sources at their pumps i.e. natural gas, propane, etc. What resulted was heavy price increases in car gasoline and home oil heating. This also influenced other industries accordingly, such as petrochemicals, transportation, clothing, etc. to the point where they had to raise their prices as well. This drove the country further into more inflation, affecting seriously the poor and those on fixed income.

It wouldn't be fair to blindly allow conventional thinking to have its' way here without at least exploring other possibilities on what happened. One other possibility occurs to me, at least concerning this windfall opportunity, which just so happened to the oil industry. The thinking on the subject argues, the OPEC crisis was a brain-child of the American oil interests, acting as a monopoly, and not caused alone by OPEC on its' own. The argument offers some convincing facts, which show that the American oil industry would gain many benefits as a result of the foreign oil cartel. One, the much fought over Alaskan Pipe Line would be approved by the US government (and was); two, due to the control of the oil supply, many of the small independents would be driven out of business (and they were); three, bans against off-shore drilling would be lifted (and they were), and of course prices at the pump would rise without controls (and they did).

The good part for the oil industry is: all this can be blamed on the infamous Arabs and their buddies, who became the fall guys with the American public. Were they really to blame, or were they in on it with the American companies? Not a bad theory. Whether you believe it or not, the fact remains, all involved in the oil industry worldwide, began making big money, and we, the consumers, are shelling out at the pump with a gun to our heads, saying take it or leave it. With all the money, we (the consumers) give them, there is no innovation coming out of the oil industry with a better (less polluting) product or alternative source of energy. Neither the cartel nor the oil refineries have come up with any really significant practical answers, because neither of them are driven to do so. Here, manipulating supply is extremely beneficial for both, and there is no one to intervene for the consumer. The American oil refineries and OPEC can control the supply of the most important energy source used by modern mankind.

Food is the second key industry in the hierarchy, which is high up on the list; perhaps one or two depending on how you look at it. Certainly, without food, survival is impossible. Additionally, motor vehicles are needed in order for commerce to function, and transportation together with commerce puts bread on the table. What goes around, comes around. How the consumer balances the two, together with his other needs is open for evaluation, and is done so in market research. The consumer has options open to him. He doesn't have to eat expensive food, or invest in an expensive car, or buy expensive clothes, and so forth and so on, depending on his disposable income, which we will address throughout the paper. Returning to food, these commodities compared to automobiles, have different steps in going to market. My guess they would take a path to the consumers something like the following: 1. the farmer, 2. the wholesaler, 3. the transporter, 4. the packager, and 5. the retailer. The one major difference, aside from how it's created, is storage life. However, it could be argued that cars have to be moved as well, but a head of lettuce doesn't have much shelf life, not as much as a Buick. The interesting fact about food is, anywhere along the way, as it goes to market, prices can be controlled through agreement of the parties concerned in the step. For example, if the farmer wants to increase the cost of his produce, he and other large farming corporations, as a group, can turn back or destroy a percentage of the product in order to do so. A case in point happened in 1974, when farmers grouped together and slaughtered a sizeable percentage of their beef calves. The farmers claimed that the price received at market, wouldn't cover the cost of raising the animal. This was because of the high cost of feed; one farming industry harming the other by inflating the price of their product. Since the going price in the market place for their beef was so low, it wasn't worth their efforts in taking it to sale. All that was left, was to slaughter them, or so they said.

The food middle men can also inflate prices. Not by controlling supply alone, but by controlling production, which sets the price, i.e. canning, packaging, bottling, etc. Food, as mentioned before, is an item in the hierarchy of needs, none can do without. In an affluent society such as ours, where Americans are used to not only ample supplies of it, but "junk foods" as well, the demand is even higher. So, there is a certain price elasticity with food products, which gives the producers the upper hand in marketing them. The orange juice producers can always say every winter that the frost has harmed their oranges, and as a result they have to raise their prices accordingly. Once they do it, it never goes back down again. Other producers can do something similar in raising prices. The trick is, they operate collectively, deciding in one of these pacts to put ceilings on the vegetables, meats or fruits which they bid on from farmers. This is equivalent to price fixing, which is difficult to prove, and who is going to do it anyway, our Chief Executive's Attorney General? I don't think so, and what court would convict them if he did? Regardless of the farmer's costs and overhead, they would receive only a certain amount from the buyers. A similar agreement can take place among the retail chains. This usually is influenced by local conditions in the market place, but results in the same phenomena of controlling and fixing prices nationwide. Here competition is greatly impaired, and inflation under the right conditions can occur.

Another important industry is housing. The prices here are mainly influenced by the interest rate for borrowing money, which is determined by government fiscal and monetary policy. Now this isn't price fixing, even though it has something to do with what the housing industry can charge for a property. Simply put, it is what the buyer can borrow to pay for a house or property. This is the way it works: if the country is in an inflationary period, the government through the Federal Reserve (or Fed) will increase interest rates on borrowing money. This high interest will filter down through the banking industry, and cause higher rates at all lending institutions throughout the country. This policy makes money tight due to the high cost of borrowing it, and holds back excessive spending, which is a major reason for inflation. This all sounds well and good, and will work directly on the problem, provided demand is the cause of the rising prices. If it is something else, say the rising cost of building supplies, then the restraints will take longer to accomplish, but should succeed as fewer houses are constructed, leaving large surpluses of these building supplies on hand. Now you say the lowering of the number of houses built, will lower supply, and that means raising prices. It does, but only in the short run.

However, as the controls begin to kick in, so does the desired price stability.

This inflationary control or cutting back, as I said, influences other industries as well, relating to and not relating to housing, causing a deceleration of the overall economy. Production rates in many industries will slow down, which generates unemployment, with decreased buying and selling. Consequently, as previously concluded, there is a lessening of demand and rising prices. It does not end there. If all things were as they should be, it would. The Empire is in a free enterprise economic system, and as such is influenced by the main flaw of such a system: monopolies. They do creep into the economy, and must be reckoned with accordingly. The government can do it with price controls, if the Democrats are in power. If the Republicans are in charge, they won't interfere, because of caveat emptor. For instance, we will say the Republicans are in power, and look at the situation from this perspective. What happens here is the monopoly itself controls prices, because they realize what inflation is doing to the economy. This ultimately impacts peoples' lives and the conduction of business. Destroy this, and we're all out in the cold. The monopoly will continue to raise prices to keep their profits, where they want them to be. Here, what results is a thing called "stagflation," a term coined by economists to describe this highly unusual situation of a recession during an inflationary period.

This stagflation is not only caused by tight money, but also by the crazed inflationary thinking of business leaders, which is almost fear motivated. It pits one industry against another trying to keep abreast of price increases. For example, when the country had the energy crunch of the late seventies, the American people responded to the president's request, and cut their use of energy products. As an outcome of their patriotic efforts, they were slapped with increased prices for home heating oil and automobile gasoline at the pumps. The reason for this, as pointed out earlier, was the diminishing of demand under a monopolistic industry which doesn't have the same effect as that of a freely competitive market. The monopoly will react differently, since they aren't immediately influenced by what is going on in the market place. As previously noted, this goes on, until the monopoly itself realizes what they are doing isn't working, and adjusts their prices to fit the economic needs of all concerned. What added to the problem back in the seventies was, the Administration sat back, and labored under the mistaken impression that the monopolies didn't exist, or if they did, were afraid to go after them, and took no action to oppose their price gouging. The anti-trust laws weren't invoked; not even a warning was given to them. Instead the president took the problem to the American people, and they wound up paying more, because the monopolies arrogantly defied them, and raised prices. This was the very thing not needed at the time for the overall health of the economy.

Another way of lessening supply is to trade it away to another nation. An example is the Soviet Union wheat deal of 1974, which started the food prices spiraling upward. What happened was, the Department of Agricultural under the Nixon Administration approved the sale of about one third of American wheat crops to Communist Russia. It was a prelude to improving relations and trade with this country and limiting the arms race. Although a good idea in the effort to limit hostilities between the powers, the plan wasn't thought out in its' entirety. It immediately caused the price of wheat in the United States to rise, and when this occurred the price of livestock also rose, since the main feed for these animals is wheat grain. The plan would have been better served, if the farmers were encouraged in advance to plant additional crops of the food i.e. raise supply. Granted the situation with the USSR may have been at a crisis level at the time, but poor planning is what it is. The situation should have never reached this point in the first place.

A second example of a food product being traded away is sugar to the same Soviet Union. This, once more, reduced a key food product's supply, and therefore forced prices up for this commodity and related foods, which are made from sugar i.e. candy, certain dry cereals, soft drinks, etc. Another example of such foreign trades was the bumper sale of our cotton crop to Japan, which drove up the price of clothing made from cotton. Levi Strauss raised their price of blue jeans by fifty percent, and you know how Americans feel about their dungarees. They paid the prices.

Now you may ask, why does the Department of Agriculture permit this burden on supply? To answer this question, it might be helpful to identify which political party was in power at the time. If it was the Republicans, then they would have a tendency to want larger and wider markets for big business, and the opening of foreign markets to improve our balance of payments. I'm not complaining about this, but if markets are expanding, shouldn't supply also be expanding? With the examples just mentioned, in order to keep prices stable, the farmers should have, in advance, planted more of their product to allow for the increased demand. I know this is repetitious, but planning is a good practice. Call it price controls, if you want, and in a way it is, but what else can be done to keep the country out of harmful inflation?

It's seldom a Republican president would ever use controls. The very ideology of this party is to govern the least possible, and allow the market place to dictate prices. The GOP would tend to permit the natural forces of the economy to evolve in order to correct itself, as mentioned earlier. The Soviet Union wheat deal is a good example of this theory. Allow the farmers to respond to this as they will, and fill the need on their own, then the economy will adjust itself quite nicely. Sounds good on paper, but that's not what takes place in the real world. Producing more doesn't necessarily mean maximizing profits, and farmers know this. Whether this large purchase will be occurring on a regular basis, must also be considered. Or, will the USSR go elsewhere to get their wheat in the future? Clearly with such an enormous wheat purchase, something should have been worked out in advance to stabilize the American market. After all, isn't this the reason, why the Department of Agriculture was created in the first place?

Now this hands off approach to the economy isn't always a Republican policy, especially when a large corporation is in trouble. Take as an example, the Chrysler Motors Corporation, whose sales had dropped off drastically in the nineteen seventies. As with many oligopolies, such as Chrysler, they came under bad management. It is difficult to know what their thought pattern was. It certainly wasn't aimed at the future, and what could happen with the price of gasoline going through the roof. The company and the other two firms, which rounded off the big three in the United States, continued on the path of manufacturing large, gas burning cars. Of note should be the fact that the foreign competition did not continue making large, gas burning cars (especially the Japanese and Koreans). Foreign automakers with their plant tooling were producing quality smaller cars all along. Consequently they had the jump on the American companies, when the oil crisis came on the scene. Regardless of ideology, the Republican administration wouldn't allow a company like Chrysler to go under, nor should they. The troubled company, under better management, responded favorably to the bailout, got back on their feet, and paid off their loan to Uncle Sam. Here in the twenty first century, the same company is back in trouble again for the same reason: bad management. It begs the question, when does the government pull the plug on them? There is another question. Is socialism creeping into the Empire's economy?

I'm going to leave these two questions for another time, and address another problem, which added to the economic difficulties of that time. Workers' salaries and wages weren't rising with the pace of inflation. This diminished disposable income (or D.I.), and had an immediate effect on the hierarchy list of spending, then and today as well. This, together with Chrysler's bad management practices in competing with foreign car imports, put them in a near bankruptcy situation. I'm using Chrysler, as an example, but other companies were in the same predicament, across the various industries. Here is what the Empire (through systems' consultants) did to adjust this lessening of buying power. One, they encouraged the hiring of women workers, since companies didn't have to pay them as much as their sexual counterpart, and two they discouraged the use of older workers, since their wages were higher than younger employees'. As with many American managers in the Empire, they have a tendency to be impressed with short term solutions, which look good on paper, but aren't. What came out of this was two income families, and older (yet capable workers) on pensions, Medicare and Social Security. Thus, companies are run by younger inexperienced people, who don't know what they are doing. Since Americans want what they want, when they want it, they turned to credit and credit card usage to get it. Inflation kept growing, and debt spending continued to grow, until the economy couldn't take it any longer.

Now there is one important problem with the Empire's decision to use discrimination as the answer to the disposable income issue in the American economy. It is not quality motivated. It promotes unqualified people into key management roles, and this disheartens innovators by the very nature of the limitations. Of course, it is no longer free; it is restricted and controlled. We can expect more bad management from American enterprises. Will it change? Change is the one constant in life. It will, but to what?

Now with every system, there is the, "all things being equal, "qualification to take under consideration. When I was a business college student, Supply and Demand consideration was mainly domestic. Today this isn't so. America's empire status has elevated its' economy to worldwide. Large US companies no longer depend entirely or mainly on the American consumer. A good percentage of its' sales come from abroad. These companies can recover before jobs in the States recover, so the economy can appear on paper to be gaining, when the average American isn't. Will the average American recover? Maybe he won't; maybe this is the future, a shrinking American middle class.

In closing my partner and I realize our description of the empire's economy is complicated and subject to change according to what power (i.e. Democrats or Republicans) is steering the ship. The Democrats could put in government price controls and invoke the Anti-trust Laws; the Republic leadership isn't likely to do this. There is no short, uncomplicated way to describe the American economy. Just when you think you know everything there is to know about it, you realize you know very little. The study of it is a very humbling experience. There is a simple approach the leadership (government and business alike) can take to help it work; it is called ethics. Yes Abraham Lincoln was right: "honesty is the best policy."

Events of the early part of the new century reveal a serious departure from honesty and moral behavior from the leadership of mega sized corporations. This has led the country into a serious economic decline; hampered further by a

Government leadership, which allowed them to continue on this way, until it reached a crisis level. If the economy is to work, the various leaderships within it must lead with an ethical drive, as part of their agenda. This way of thinking develops trust between the various industries within the system, and filters down to the employees, customers and investors. Beyond this, there is no pure scientific plan in running the economy. That's why, when it goes bad, it may take a long time to get it right again.

(20)Source: Economics An Introductory Analysis by Paul A. Samuelson, Fifth Edition, McGraw-Hill Book Company, Inc., New York, 1961

End of: SUPPLY AND DEMAND

EPILOGUE

To repeat from our Opening Statement, my partner and I wrote The American Empire in essay form in order to isolate each step, which brought the United States from a country to an empire status. The steps, we concluded, occurred in approximately the past fifty years. When beginning the work, we didn't anticipate where the research would take us, and the surprising conclusion of it. Allow me to lead up to this before sharing our findings. The problem with world dominance is the great responsibility which comes with the administering and controlling such a vast undertaking. The Empire must direct their own people as well as the peoples of the world. The USA does this with the world's largest Navy and Air Force, which is backed by the largest defense budget. This gives the Empire a strong striking force anywhere in the world. In addition the Empire has troops permanently stationed in key countries on every continent, ready to be deployed at a moment's notice. This comes at a price, a money price. All this was documented in our first book, Everything You Should Know About The World's Environment, But Are Indifferent To Ask!

There are two ways of getting money: one, earning it, and two, saving it. Let's look at it from "earning" it. The Empire doesn't earn money; it taxes to get money, and secondly, it borrows money. (2)The following are their receipts by source: individual income taxes, corporate income taxes, social insurances and retirement receipts, excise taxes, estate and gift taxes, customs duties and fees, and miscellaneous receipts. I'm not going to list the outlays, since there are so many of them; you can look them up, if you are interested. But only to say the defense budget is quite large, second only to the social security budget. Now if receipts don't cover outlays (or expenses), then the Empire has to borrow money from the open lending market, which can affect interest rates, etc. and the debt can keep going, since debt must be paid; money isn't free. Now the second way of earning money is by saving it. No, the Empire doesn't cut administrative expenses, because that would mean doing away with or limiting bureaucrats, which is out of the question. I don't know, why. What the Empire does in place of savings, is to broaden the tax base. They can do that in several ways, which I mentioned before, but feel it is important enough to mention again. One, they can refrain from spending. The infrastructures of America's major highways and bridges are beginning to show signs of neglect and wear. Secondly, to be soft on crime. There is a serious shortage of police protection in the large cities and on roads and highways from aggressive drivers. Many criminals have money, and make investments with it; the profits of which the Empire can tax, if the criminals are not in jail. The way the Empire knows they have money is apparent when they are charged with a crime, and come before the courts. If they are represented with a prestigious defense attorney, then they know the accused has money. You recall the old saying, "rich people don't go to jail". They don't. The criminals are walking the streets making money, driving expensive SUV's, and paying taxes. The slogan to explain this policy persists, "who said life has to be fair." Does someone have to answer this for it to happen?

Or, does the nobility of mankind and his search for justice imply that indeed, life should be fair?

To get to the point of our findings with the book, there is a serious correlation between what the average American lost with their civil liberties, and the growth and expansion of the American Empire. No, America is not a better place to live in than, when I was a young man. The reason is, the Empire is trying to do too much. They can't serve their public and administer protection and justice on their behalf, and at the same time control the world. The Empire is now making a decision, who they favor more between the two. We have given our opinion concerning the direction this decision has taken, and backed it up with proof and facts. The truth is difficult to accept, we know, especially when it goes against our homeland; the land we cherish. However, the truth will set you free. For this reason alone, we conclude: it is better to know, than not to know.
(2)Source: TIME Almanac, 2003

End of: B. J. & A. C.'S ESSAYS

(THE AMERICAN EMPIRE)

BIBLIOGRAPHY (1)

The World Almanac and Books of Facts,
Copyrighted 1998 by PRIMEDIA Reference, Inc. –
World Almanac Books, Mahwah, New Jersey – a
PRIMEDIA   Company

(2) TIME Almanac 2003 with Information
Please – Information Please, Boston, MA – a part
of Family Education Network, Inc. – TIME Inc.
Home Entertainment – Copyrighted 2002 by
Family Education Network, Inc.
(2a) The Justice Policy Institute 2002
(2b) Prisoners in 2000, U. S. Bureau of Justice
Statistics

(3) Good News Bible – Catholic Study
Edition – Sadlier, A division of William H. Sadlier,
Inc., New York, Chicago, Los Angeles

(4) Parade Magazine – The Sunday
Newspaper Magazine (1/14/07)
Parade Publications, 711 Third Avenue, New York,
NY 10017

(5) The Concise Columbia Encyclopedia, Second Edition – Columbia   University Press, New York – Doubleday Book & Music Clubs, Inc., Garden City, New York – Copyrighted 1989 by Columbia University Press

(6) Bonnie & Clyde – Wikipedia, the free encyclopedia, 9/26/09.   Wikipedia® is a registered trademark of the Wikimedia Foundation, Inc., a non-profit organization.

(7) This Ring Surf Old West Net ring, owned by Butch and Sundance in Bolivia 9/26/09

(8) Capitalizing on an Aging Workforce by Ken Nogan, Risk Control Consultant at PMA Insurance Group in a quarterly series by the PMA Companies called PMA Insights.
(8a) Safe Workplace & Safety News; Older Workers Mean Greater Safety & Productivity – 9/1909.

(9) Dow Jones year ending closing averages. The Dow Jones Statistics–N.Y. Times

End of Year Quotes, Copyrighted by the N.Y. Times each year, Delaware County Library System.

(10) The original Pledge of Allegiance was published 9/8/1892 issue of the Youth's Companion in Boston, MA, credited to Francis Bellamy of the magazine's staff.
(10a) The phrase "under God" was added to the pledge on June 14, 1954.

(11) The American Nation – a History of the United States by John A. Garraty – Columbia University – Harper & Row, Publisher, Incorporated, American Heritage Publishing Co., Inc., New York and London – Copyrighted 1966.

(12) Wikipedia, the free encyclopedia – Earl Warren and the Warren Commission – 11/2/09. Wikipedia® is a registered trademark of the Wikimedia Foundation, Inc., a non-profit organization.

(13) NNDB tracking the entire world – Nancy Reagan 11/9/09 – Nancy Reagan

Bibliography - National First Ladies Library -
Ronald Reagan Presidential Foundation & Library
11/9/09.

(14) Reaganomics, from Wikipedia, the free
encyclopedia -11/16/09.
Wikipedia® is a registered trademark of the
Wikimedia Foundation, Inc., a non-profit
organization.

(15) National Highway Traffic Safety
Administration - 2006.

(16) Safe Car Guide.com Inc., Inc. a coach
built.com affiliate.   Copyrighted 2009.

(17) SUV Rollover Statistics, sponsored by
the Newsome Law Firm - Orlando, Florida, who
represents consumers injured by defective
products.

(18) Port Authority of New York and New
Jersey, and TIME Magazine.

(19) LIFE Sixty Years, by the Editor of Life

Magazine, a Sixtieth Anniversary Celebration 1936 – 1996. Published by LIFE Books, TIME Inc., New York, NY – Copyrighted 1996, Time Inc. Home Entertainment.

(20) Economics – An Introductory Analysis, by Paul A. Samuelson, Professor of Economics, Massachusetts Institute of Technology, Publisher, McGraw–Hill Book Company, Inc., New York, NY, 1961